BUSINESS
MODELS

Additional Titles in Entrepreneur's Made Easy Series

Entrepreneur MAGAZINE'S

BUSINESS MODELS

made easy

Entrepreneur Press and Don Debelak

Ep Entrepreneur. Press

Editorial Director: Jere Calmes
Cover Design: Beth Hansen-Winter
Editorial and Production Services: CWL Publishing Enterprises, Inc., Madison, Wisconsin, www.cwlpub.com

This publication is designed to provide accurate and authoritative information in regard to the subject matter covered. It is sold with the understanding that the publisher is not engaged in rendering legal, accounting, or other professional services. If legal advice or other expert assistance is required, the services of a competent professional person should be sought.

—From a Declaration of Principles jointly adopted by a Committee of the American Bar Association and a Committee of Publishers and Associations

ISBN 1-59918-041-3

Library of Congress Cataloging-in-Publication Data
Debelak, Don.
  Business models made easy / by Entrepreneur Press and Don Debelak.
    p. cm.
  ISBN 1-59918-041-3 (alk. paper)
  1. Business planning. I. Entrepreneur Press. II. Title.
  HD30.28.D3965 2006
  658.4'01dc22

2006020657

11 10 09 08 07 06   10 9 8 7 6 5 4 3 2 1

Printed in Canada

Contents

Preface

OVER THE PAST 20 YEARS I'VE WORKED WITH DOZENS OF NEW businesses putting together plans and strategies and doing feasibility analyses of their proposed ventures. I've become increasingly aware over the years that people like to follow the business plan format, starting with an executive summary and covering all aspects of the business from management to production, without really evaluating the feasibility of their concept.

As I write this book in the summer of 2006 it is becoming obvious that business owners face great challenges launching a new business. Competition is fierce and consumers are harder to reach today than ever before. Small to mid-sized business owners struggle to make a market impact. They don't just need a business plan; they need a great concept that will generate sustainable profits.

Companies that succeed today, either on purpose or by accident, have created a business model that delivers what I call the GEL factors for success: Great customers, Easy sales, and Long life. The goal of this book is to first show you what a business model is, then show how to evaluate and fine-tune that business model by use of the GEL factor analysis, and finally show how to write a great business plan based on a winning business model.

The Format

The book is divided into two sections, the first on evaluating a business model, which I call the GEL factor analysis, and the second on how to write a business plan. The first section is divided into three parts. The first explains what a business model is with Chapter 3 outlining the business models for 18 companies. The second part explains how to do a GEL factor analysis to evaluate your business model, with an eye to determining if a model is worth pursuing and how you can improve your model if it seems to pass this evaluation. The final section is a GEL factor analysis for a variety of businesses to give you a better understanding of how the system works.

In the business plan section of the book I've included two plans, one that I use throughout the business plan chapters to show how the advice in those chapters can be executed. The second plan is an example of how a plan is written when an entrepreneur is trying to raise money. These plans are not overly long but offer a succinct look at each company's philosophy, business model, and implementation plan.

Writing the Plan

I've written dozens of business plans. Great plans always start with an analysis of your business or business concept. The reason you write a plan is that it forces you to reevaluate your business. When people tell me they haven't written a plan for three or four years, they usually justify the absence of a plan on the fact that their business hasn't changed. I believe what they are telling me is that they are flying by the seat of their pants. Everyone's business changes every year—and often every six months. Customers, competition, and distribution are all changing and an entrepreneur who doesn't reevaluate his or her business is taking a real chance that their business might fail. Entrepreneurs should do a plan every year.

Tips and Stories

Throughout the book you'll find four boxes, each offering different types of information.

1. **Definitions of words and jargon.** Concepts that are frequently used in venture capital and entrepreneur circles but that are not always well-known by current or future small business owners.
2. **Company stories.** Each chapter in the business model section includes a story about a company that used the tactic highlighted in the chapter.

These stories should help you see that average companies are transforming their businesses every year. Plus, I hope the stories give you a better understanding of how companies have used their creativity to find a wide variety of strategies to make their businesses successful.

3. **Insights.** Some sidebar boxes give you answers to the questions business owners commonly ask me, such as "How do I set my prices?" or "How much will I need to introduce a product or service?"

3. **GEL Factors.** These are listed next to every story about a company and will rate the business being discussed. A "yes," "no," or "average" listed after each of the three letters, G, E and L, means the company either has Great customers, Easy sales, or Long life or it doesn't, or the companies' situation is average, which is a middle-of-the-road rating. The medallions should help you start to analyze companies by these three critical factors.

G—Yes
E—No
L—Average

I had three goals in writing this book. First, I want to give you a new way to look at your business idea or your current business to find strategies that could dramatically improve your sales and profit. Second, I want to help you realize a business plan can be more than just a tool for raising money or for creating a budgeting process: it can be a tool that reevaluates and strategically positions your business every year. Third, I want to offer you new skills for managing your strategic planning process.

Good luck, and most of all, good planning! I encourage you not to rush through the book, but to take your time to formulate your own winning model and plan as you read the book. Your future depends on it.

Don Debelak
DSD Marketing
P.O. Box 120861
New Brighton, MN 55112
www.dondebelak.com
dondebelak@dondebelak.com

Section 1
Part One

Business Models:
Developing an Understanding

Chapter 1

Business Models— A Definition

From Wikipedia, the Internet's free encyclopedia

Abusiness model (also called a business design) is the instrument by which a business intends to generate revenue and profits. It is a summary of how a company means to serve its employees and customers, and involves both strategy (what a business intends to do) as well as an implementation (how the business will carry out its plans).

THE BIGGEST PROBLEM WITH WRITING A BOOK TITLED *BUSINESS Models Made Easy* is that no single accepted definition of business models has really emerged. For decades terms like the *razor blade business model*, where you sell a product for a low value and cash in on the consumable sales, have been used for years. Other terms, like the *application service provider* (ASP), model were big in the dotcom era, where an ASP hosted complex software on its site and allowed customers to use it for a monthly fee.

But discussing those models doesn't get to the nature of what a business model really is. Another way to get at the definition of business model is to look at why people, particularly banks and investors, often mention business models—because it is easier to evaluate a business' potential with a business model than with a business plan. Most people can't articulate clearly what they feel is the business model, and often they just say they don't like the model when they see something in a business concept that they don't agree with. So the purpose of the business model concept for investors and bankers is a quick way to evaluate a business. People developing a business concept should apply the same reasoning—they need a quick and easy way to evaluate their concept to see if it will work, or to see how it can be modified in order for it to succeed.

Easy to Understand and Use

Despite the lack of a consistent, recognized definition of business model, I've found that most of the people I've known, and most of the articles I've read discussing the business model concept deal with the following six elements when deciding if the company has a good business model. When all six of these elements are favorable, then you have a good business model. The Great Customers, Easy Sales, and Long Life (GEL) factor analysis, discussed in Chapter 4, offers a way for you to understand when your concept meets the favorable test for each of the six elements, and how to adjust your concept if it doesn't.

The purpose of the business model concept for investors and bankers is a quick way to evaluate a business.

1. Acquire high value customers—favorable condition: without spending a lot of money.
2. Offer significant value to customers—favorable condition: having a significant competitive advantage.
3. Deliver products or services with high margins—favorable condition: with high quality and few opportunities for error.
4. Provide for customer satisfaction—favorable condition: service and training, if needed, provided by someone else.
5. Maintaining market position—favorable condition: market position is protected or a steady stream of new products or services can be maintained.
6. Funding the business—favorable condition: investments reasonable for market size and risk both for start-up costs and for market maintenance.

I like to consider the six key elements as being three green and three red lights. The first three points, acquiring high value customers, offering significant value, and delivering products and services at high margins are three positive elements you need to go ahead. You have them in place and you have the green lights. The last three points, providing for customer satisfaction, maintaining market position, and funding are areas where a business model can run into a red light. The business model stops working if product support is difficult, if you don't have a good method of maintaining your market position, or if the business model requires too much investment. So a great business model delivers big time on the green lights and avoids the red. Add the green lights and avoid the red and you have a "can't miss" business model.

> ## Insight
>
> Though you will understand business models after reading this book, most of the people you talk to will not, so as you are developing your model look for other companies that work under a similar model. Then when you are asked about your model tell people it is similar to that company's, and then explain your model.

A successful business model, however, is only the first checkpoint on the way to a good business plan. Once you have a model, the rest of your plan, management, marketing strategy, strengths, and weaknesses all still matter. So you need a good start with the model, followed by a thorough business plan that takes advantage of your model and helps create the management team and staff necessary to implement the plan. Then you have success. But everything still starts with a winning model.

You need a good start with the model, followed by a thorough business plan that takes advantage of your model and helps create the management team and staff necessary to implement the plan.

Green Lights

Acquiring High Value Customers

High value customers doesn't mean rich customers, but customers who

- ▶ Are easy to locate
- ▶ Allow you to charge a profitable price
- ▶ Are willing to try your product after minimal marketing expenses
- ▶ Can generate enough business to meet your sales and profit objectives

Customers don't necessarily need to be the end users of your product or service, they could be retailers, distributors, catalogs, or whoever you sell your product or service to. If your end users or distributors don't fit this profile, you still could be able to meet this requirement by attracting high value customers through partnerships or alliances with other companies in the market.

Offer Significant Value to Customers

People typically think in terms of competitive advantage related to features and benefits as significant value, but there are a number of ways you can create value besides maintaining a competitive advantage. They include providing:

- Unique advantages in features and benefits;
- Better distribution through retail or distribution;
- More complete customer solutions through alliances with other companies;
- Lower pricing due to manufacturing efficiencies or pricing options; and
- Faster delivery, broader product line, or offering customers more options for customization.

*B*usiness today is nothing like it was 20 or even 10 years ago where product features were the prominent ways people added value to customers.

Business today is nothing like it was 20 or even 10 years ago where product features were the prominent ways people added value to customers. The rise of the Internet and outsourcing, but most of all the increased willingness of companies to partner in creative ways to serve customers, has resulted in every industry creating innovation in business strategy. This gives you opportunities, but also makes it imperative that you stay on the creative edge to fend off competition.

Insight

It is very difficult for small businesses or entrepreneurs to compete against significantly larger businesses as a minimum of a 25 or even 50 percent advantage is necessary to succeed. A break-through product like a Garlic Twist, rather than a garlic press, has that advantage, but more than likely an improved garlic press won't. You can get by with less of an advantage if you face small competitors. One additional key to look for is that your customers immediately spot your advantage. Don't count on an advantage that is hard to notice.

Deliver Products or Services with High Margins

Better manufacturing costs due to overseas manufacturing is typically not the clear way to higher margins, as competitors will often match your costs in the end. Higher margins come from having a product that can be made from an improved process or by having high value features that provide significant value that allow you to charge more. But you can achieve high margins with other tactics including:

- ▸ Having a more efficient distribution channel
- ▸ Requiring less sales support and sales effort
- ▸ Having an industry-leading, lean manufacturing process
- ▸ Offering more auxiliary products or other opportunities for revenue without increasing sales costs

Delivering products or services with high margins seems like it is an obvious concern for every business. It certainly has been a concern for at least the 35 years that I've been in business. But it seems that the business models and business plans I've seen over the last few years do not have enough time spent on delivering high margin products and services despite its being a bedrock principle in every successful business model. That is a big mistake, as often your significant value can come out of your ability to achieve high margins.

Red Lights

Provide for Customer Satisfaction

This is the start of the business model red lights. The question is: Will it be difficult (and therefore expensive) to satisfy customers once they buy? Some of the aspects of a business that create high customer satisfaction costs include:

- ▸ Having good warranty policies
- ▸ Maintaining extensive technical support
- ▸ Easy installation either through simplicity of the product or by the assistance of a support staff
- ▸ Maintaining extensive customer service
- ▸ Interfacing easily with other equipment or dealing quickly with interface problems

An ideal model uses a company's resources to add customers and create customer value.

In a sense, a business model determines resource allocation. An ideal model uses a company's resources to add customers and create customer value, which improves a company's market position and adds value to a company, and uses few resources to produce products and services and maintain customer satisfaction. Customer satisfaction costs, which occur after the sale, are red flags because the costs are typically high and don't produce revenue or profits. Maintaining customer satisfaction is only ideal when it results in your company adding value to the customer.

As in all aspects of a business model, the fact that your type of product might have high customer service costs isn't a deal stopper; you just need to configure your business to put these costs on someone else, either with partnerships or alliances, or by restricting your sales to an aspect of the business that doesn't require high costs for customer satisfaction. For example, the business I started in 2005 sells diesel particulate traps, which are part of a diesel emission system. Dealing with a new product to truck and bus fleets requires lots of technical support, follow-up maintenance, and customer service. We have chosen to sell the filter only to system integrators that take on the costs of customer satisfaction of fleets. We still need to keep our integrators happy, but that is much easier to do as we have fewer customers and far fewer problems.

Maintaining Market Position

A good business model uses its resources to improve its market position, adding new products, features, and customers or expanding into new applications.

A good business model uses its resources to improve its market position, adding new products, features, and customers or expanding into new applications. A business cannot do that if it has to constantly fight for market position, either with price discounts to major customers, or by absorbing the costs of trading customers with competitors. Patent protection, brand names, customer loyalty, and unique value in the market are ways companies strengthen market position. But there are red flags to watch for that indicate a model could be in trouble, including:

▶ Two or three major customers buy most of your product

▶ Major potential competitors control the distribution network

▶ Technology changes rapidly and requires high-risk product development

▶ There are alternative technologies being developed to meet the same need

▶ You have well-funded potential competitors who could quickly move into your market

There is an old adage that people can't see the forest for the trees. Often entrepreneurs fall into that trap, looking at the details of their business without understanding the overall market landscape, and the features of that landscape can cause them trouble. Long term, your ability to hold market position is determined by the characteristics of the overall market. For example, I worked for a company in the semiconductor manufacturing business. New technology constantly was being developed, some that worked with our product and some that didn't. We were a small company, and guessing right on every technology change, something we had to do to hold market position, was just too difficult.

Funding the Business

Start-up costs, operating capital, personnel and overhead costs are just a small percentage of the funding requirements for any business. The question is whether or not the investments will have a high return, and whether or not the business can grow without substantial new investments. Drug companies might have a high initial investment for R&D in a new drug, but then after that investment is made a drug can be sold at a high profit for years. Service businesses, on the other hand, may require substantial investments for all expanded sales dollars. Red flags for a business model regarding investments include:

- ▶ ROI (return of investment) is less than 25 percent in the first three years
- ▶ Incremental production of products or services requires substantial additional investments
- ▶ Less than 50 percent of the investment required will be used in revenue-producing areas (sales and production)
- ▶ Investments have to be made prior to sales commitments
- ▶ Industry as a whole has a poor ROI or poor profitability

New entrepreneurs tend to think money will be hard to come by and often put together a business model that requires little money, outsourcing all production as an example, but then don't leave enough room in their pricing to generate profits. Money is available for the right plan and the right model. Always start with the investments you need for your most efficient business model. You'll find money available if your ROI is right and if you have financial leverage, which means your initial investment will allow you to double or triple sales without requiring any more funding.

You'll find money available if your ROI is right and if you have financial leverage, which means your initial investment will allow you to double or triple sales without requiring any more funding.

9

Chapter 2

Creating Your Business Model

F or investors, a business model is a way to evaluate whether a business will succeed. But for an entrepreneur, it is a tool to create a dynamic business. A successful entrepreneur starts by preparing an initial model and then looking it over, seeing what works and what doesn't, and then changing the model. A model is not a pass-or-fail test to the entrepreneur; it is a building block that leads him or her to a strong, profitable business.

M ANY ENTREPRENEURS TELL ME THAT THEY DON'T HAVE A BUSIness model. But that is not true: every business has a model, whether it has been chosen directly or is just the result of how your business is set up. Every business deals in some way with our six key elements, whether you are an at-home business, retailer, small service provider, or big manufacturer. Your business must be able to effectively provide all of the following elements or it will quickly fail:

- ▶ Acquiring customers
- ▶ Offering value to customers
- ▶ Delivering products or services with high margins

- ▶ Providing customer satisfaction
- ▶ Maintaining market position
- ▶ Funding the business

Your goal is to create your business model intentionally and with goals in mind. You want to make sure you start with a model that looks promising. In Chapter 5, you will be evaluating your model, fine-tuning it as needed to be sure it is effective. In this chapter, you will fill in your model's starting point. To help you understand each section, I've included the business model for Chatterbox, Inc., a company that supplies paper, borders, templates, and other products used by scrapbook enthusiasts to create the perfect scrapbook. When you are doing your own model, you should start with the strategy chosen for each element and then include the options you have not chosen, so that you are have a ready Option B if your strategy doesn't score well in the GEL factor analysis. The Chatterbox example in this chapter lists both the strategy chosen and the option. Chapter 3 lists the models for 18 different businesses, but those models only list the actual strategy chosen.

As you look at the Chatterbox example, notice how it is balanced with the resources it had available. For example, the company didn't want to borrow money or obtain loans, and its target market of scrapbook stores, a small market compared to mass merchandisers, requires much smaller investments. For a model to work, the elements need to have both favorable conditions and be balanced, with all elements working together.

Acquire Customers

Chatterbox

A. Target Customers: Scrapbook enthusiasts that spend a minimum of $1,000 per year on scrapbook supplies
Other options:
 1. Casual, but experienced scrapbook enthusiasts
 2. People not currently scrapbooking
B. Target Distribution: Scrapbook stores and hobby shops
Other options:
 1. Photography stores
 2. Mass merchandisers
 3. Craft stores (such as Michaels)

C. Attract Customer Attention: (1) wide distribution, (2) frequent product introductions along with press release programs, (3) small ads in key magazines targeted at dedicated scrapbook enthusiasts
Other options:
1. Ads in more widely circulated magazines such as *Good Housekeeping*, and Mary Engelbreit's *Home Companion*
2. Promotion on shopping channels QVC, Shop NBC, and HSN to expand publicity

Insight

The ideal target customer looks to find you rather than you looking to find them. Experienced scrapbookers often work weekly or monthly with friends, have a huge network of scrapbooking cohorts, and are always visiting stores looking for the newest products. Convincing casual users to come to you is far more difficult.

Your Business

A. Target Customers: _____
Other options:
1. _____

2. _____

B. Target Distribution: _____
Other options:
1. _____

2. _____

3. _____

C. Attract Customer Attention: _____

_____

Other options:
1. _____

_____

2. _____

_____

Offer Value to Customers

Chatterbox

A. Features and Benefits: Offer coordinated packages that create 28 different page themes and formats from a small number of pages, orders, tags, and embellishments.

Other options:

1. Provide a wide number of complete kits, with one design per kit
2. Specialize in borders, an area where Chatterbox has several unique designs, then people can use the borders with other products

B. Solution Provided: Provide a complete solution for creating a variety of well-designed scrapbook pages

Other options:

1. Provide the ideal border solution, working with products from other vendors
2. Provide easier-to-use kits that make just one specific design—more ideal for casual scrapbookers

C. Pricing: Product priced about 15 percent above the market average to indicate that the product is upscale for more serious scrapbook enthusiasts

Other options:

1. Mid-range pricing to try and attract a larger audience
2. 30 percent higher pricing to generate more profit per sales from serious scrapbookers

---

Insight

Don't be afraid of a premium price. Often it is a marketing tool that separates your products or services from the competition. I think it is always best for entrepreneurs to start their plan by pricing their product 10 to 15 percent above the competition and then figure out what features and services they need to offer to justify that price. Then if they go to more of a market price, they will have more features to offer.

Your Business

A. Features and Benefits: _____

_____

Other options:

1. _____

2. _____

B. Solution Provided: _____

_____

Other options:

1. _____

2. _____

C. Pricing: _____
Other options:

1. _____

2. _____

Deliver Products or Services with High Margins

Chatterbox

A. Production Source: Products are prepared in Tennessee from readily available materials at two separate opportunity workshops
Other options:
1. Use one of three paper die cutters and have products assembled at a workshop or at a contract assembly house
2. Produce and assemble through contract manufacturing firms in Asia
B. Cost Control: Chatterbox uses multiple material suppliers, and rebids the work to four production vendors every six months
Other options:
1. Use overseas manufacturers to reduce costs
2. Consolidate production to one vendor to hopefully negotiate better pricing
C. Margin Control Through Distribution: Hobby and scrapbook dealers and distributors take much smaller markups than mass merchandisers and their distributors. Chatterbox nets 12 percent extra (over mass merchandisers) in sales through this distribution channel.

Other options:
1. Sell through mass merchandisers and use volume to try and negotiate better pricing
2. Bring on board an in-house sales team to call scrapbook stores and hobby retailers

Your Business

A. Production Source: _____

_____

Other options:

1. _____

2. _____

B. Cost Controls: _____

_____

Other options:

1. _____

2. _____

C. Margin Control Through Distribution: _____
Other options:

1. _____

2. _____

Provide Customer Satisfaction

Chatterbox

A. Quality Control: Company produces products with local companies to easily monitor production; producers have assigned one production lead for six workers to monitor quality
Other options:
1. Switch to local ISO 9000 (a nationally recognized quality standard) qualified producers; the downside is that companies with quality procedures often are more expensive
2. Use overseas production sources with quality standards
B. Training, Installation, and Technical Support: Training will be provided at trade shows and through a video geared for use in classes held at scrapbook retailers.

Other options:
1. Training for major retailers and end users at the company's web site or company headquarters
2. Rely on instructions with each package, or provide an instruction manual for each shop

C. Interface Challenges: Products are sold as stand-alone kits, with all the components, borders, stickers, templates, and other accessories to make pages with 28 different designs
   Other options:
   1. Sell only one facet of a page, or one combination of two items that can work with standard product offerings at scrapbook stores
   2. Sell complete kits that can produce a page with just one or two designs

Insight

Virtually all new product entrepreneurs take customer satisfaction for granted. In fact, it is one of the most difficult aspects of a business. You must assume things will go wrong, and then figure out how you will satisfy customers. Think of the most difficult person you know, and then figure out what his or her complaints might be and how you would resolve them.

Your Business

A. New Product Strategy: _____

_____

Other options:

1. _____

2. _____

B. Training, Installation, and Technical Support: _____

_____

Other options:

1. _____

2. _____

C. Interface Challenges: _____
   Other options:

1. _____

2. _____

Maintaining Market Position

Chatterbox

A. New Product Strategy: Use of local opportunity workshops allows company to maintain a steady stream of new products with minimal introduction costs for production
Other options:
    1. Work with paper suppliers of high-end decorative papers who can die cut new products
    2. Use overseas vendors, who are lower cost, but with higher start-up costs and costs for new products

B. Distribution Channel Control: Specialty distributors can't land the major brands and they are brand loyal to Chatterbox, which is a major line for them.
Other options:
1. Sell direct to mass merchants or large craft store chains like Michaels, although company would have little control and would be forced to offer heavy discounts
2. Hiring an in-house sales and marketing staff to sell directly to smaller retailers

C. Competitor Situation: Company avoids competing with large manufacturers by concentrating on the smaller chains and narrower distribution
Other options:
    1. Selling to mass merchants: Company would compete with larger industry competitors
    2. In-house sales staff: This strategy could open up the specialty distributors market to other small competitors

Your Business

A. New Product Strategy: _____

_____

Other options:

    1. _____

    2. _____

B. Distribution Channel Control: _____

_____

Other options:

1. _____

2. _____

C. Competitor Situation: _____
   Other options:

   1. _____

   2. _____

Funding the Business

Chatterbox

A. Initial Funding: Funding provided by personal savings and credit cards. Minimize initial funding by taking advantage of the extended terms offered by the opportunity workshops and by localizing marketing efforts in Tennessee and Georgia
   Other options:
   1. Raise money from family and friends for initial development to prove product will sell and introduce the product to a wider market
   2. Take out an SBA loan to introduce the product to a wider market along with some financing from family and friends

B. Funding Operations: Initial funding can take company to sales of $15,000 after which an SBA loan will be obtained to fund broad distribution
   Other options:
   1. Raise money from investors, family, or friends
   2. Grow at a slower rate that can be sustained by the initial company sales

C. Funding New Product Development: By using the opportunity workshops, new product development introduction costs are low as company founder can work directly with the production head to hold new product costs down and development can be funded by existing sales
   Other options:
   1. Use a design company to produce a designer line for mass merchants with funding from investment groups or an increase in the SBA loan
   2. Use overseas production to produce low-cost new products with just one to three page designs produced by each kit. SBA loans or

investors could be used to fund this new product direction.

Your Business

A. Initial Funding: _____

> ### Insight
>
> Many entrepreneurs are afraid to try to raise money, so they take the bootstrap approach. Before doing that, visit your local Small Business Development Center, *www.sba.gov/sbdc*. They can explain funding options to you and help you determine if you could get a bank loan or an investment from an angel investor.

_____

Other options:

    1. _____

    2. _____

B. Funding Operations: _____

_____

Other options:

    1. _____

    2. _____

C. Funding New Product Development: _____
Other options:

    1. _____

    2. _____

Chapter 3

Case Studies: Business Models

A business model deals with key issues regarding how a company is run that relate to acquiring customers, satisfying customers while making profits, and being able to first maintain and then grow a company's market share. Every company has a business model, whether or not they chose it deliberately, or whether or not the business founder has heard of or understands what a business model is.

THE GOAL OF THIS BOOK IS TO HELP BUSINESS OWNERS DELIBERATELY choose a model, then analyze that model to give it the best chance to succeed, and then finally to use the model to write a business plan. Established businesses might choose not to write the plan, but due to the rapidly changing market conditions, they still will find it beneficial to list and evaluate their business model once per year.

Since I've found that the term *business model* is confusing to people, I've listed business models in this chapter for six categories of businesses: retail, service, product, personal service, distribution, and Internet. I've listed in each group a small business, a mid-sized business, and a business that is struggling or has failed. I've included three ratings for each factor in the business model: **Rating +, Rating ?,** and **Rating =** (for neutral). You may not understand why an aspect of the business model received its rating now, but you will be able to understand it if you come back to review this chapter after reading the GEL (Great customers, Easy sales, and Long life) factor analysis in the following chapters. I'm also jumping the gun and listing a GEL factor rating at the beginning of each company example, with either a yes, no, or average rating for each example. This section will get you thinking about how to carefully and objectively evaluate a business model.

Retail Businesses

D Rock Landscape Supplies

Business Description: A supplier of summer landscape products to both landscape design firms and consumers. They carry decorative stone products, retaining walls, fireplace kits, wood mulch, and yard ornaments.

> G–Average
> E–Average
> L–Average

1. Acquire customers: **Rating =.** 70 percent of business is from 10 landscape designers and 30 percent retail. Two salespeople keep steady contact with current designer customers and solicit new business.
2. Offer value to customers: **Rating =.** Offer computer modeling services for designers and consumers so they can see an image of the design under consideration, offer full service on every project by sourcing items for the customer that D Rock doesn't carry.
3. Deliver products or services with high margins: **Rating +.** Margins are high for the industry due to a high level of service that improves the result of the landscaping service.
4. Provide customer satisfaction: **Rating =.** Maintained with current inventory and partnership arrangements with three other landscape supply houses to deliver the right product when needed.
5. Maintaining market position: **Rating =.** Two salespeople call on 10 major accounts and 30 others in the metro area to hold market share.
6. Funding the business: **Rating =.** Suppliers offer 90-day terms during peak summer season and company is in a financial position to fund any additional inventory needs.

Casual Male Big and Tall

Business Description: Formerly the Big and Tall store chain. They changed their name to lessen the negative stigma of the former name, and they added more casual dress, reducing their previous reliance on suits and more formal clothing. Company has stores throughout the country.

G—Average
E—Yes
L—Yes

1. Acquire customers: **Rating +.** Primarily is found by customers who search for clothes to fit them that are not available at standard retailers. Name recognition and advertising in the Yellow Pages produces a steady stream of customers.
2. Offer value to customers: **Rating +.** Offers a wide variety of choices and options to customers who otherwise can't even find clothes to fit them.
3. Deliver products or services with high margins: **Rating +.** Margins are strong as most retailers have limited, if any, selection to serve this market segment.
4. Provide customer satisfaction: **Rating +.** Satisfaction has jumped as the line of clothing has broadened to include more of the clothes its customers want.
5. Maintaining market position: **Rating +.** Market is expanding as people gain weight but not to the point it has become a lucrative market for others.
6. Funding the business: **Rating =.** Company has established stores and is able to expand as needed into new markets based on their current sales success.

True Value Hardware

Business Description: Provides products and services to neighborhood hardware stores. It doesn't own the stores, but signs a license agreement for the store to use their name and be involved in their promotions in return for the store buying goods from True Value Hardware. Small stores, with strong service, have suffered as big home improvement stores such as Home Depot and Lowes have expanded into new markets.

G—No
E—No
L—No

1. Acquire customers: **Rating ?.** New small hardware retailers are few and far between, and stealing customers from competitors like Ace Hardware is difficult.
2. Offer value to customers: **Rating ?.** Company offers an adequate product selection but is unable to create enough promotional tools to help their customer base compete against big retailers.

3. Deliver products or services with high margins: **Rating ?.** Difficulties of their customer base lead to pricing pressures on company.
4. Provide customer satisfaction. **Rating ?.** Customers want to match big retailers' prices and margins, which is difficult for the company to do for each small retailer.
5. Maintaining market position: **Rating ?.** Its customers are losing market share so company is facing an inevitable decline in the market share and it will have a difficult time reversing this trend.
6. Funding the business: **Rating =.** Funding is already in place. Funding for a major expansion or new direction might be hard to acquire.

Service Oriented

Petrykowski Realty

Business Description: A realtor partnership of mother and daughter who work jointly for their customers either to find or sell a home.

> G–Average
> E–Yes
> L–Yes

1. Acquire customers: **Rating =.** Word of mouth, open houses, and networking.
2. Offer value to customers: **Rating +.** Two people, of different ages, offer better service to customers selling homes, more hands-on attention.
3. Deliver products or services with high margins: **Rating =.** Similar to margins of most retailers.
4. Provide customer satisfaction: **Rating +.** Having two realtors offers better coverage when one of the agents is busy. Also, they deal better with vacations and other absences.
5. Maintaining market position: **Rating =.** Should be able to hold market share if they continue their high level of service.
6. Funding the business: **Rating +.** Low funding requirements once the initial licenses have been obtained and the initial promotional program run.

Daymark Solutions

Business Description: IT provider specializing in setting up company systems for backup and recovery systems. Has servers on its location for small to mid-sized companies but also specializes in setting up a complete recovery system, including servers at company locations.

> G–Yes
> E–Yes
> L–No

1. Acquire customers: **Rating =.** Relies on trade show attendance, recommendations from current accounts, a small amount of advertising, and cold calls by its sales force.
2. Offer value to customers: **Rating +.** Companies realize more and more the value of backup security and Daymark has had an established reputation for multiple years.
3. Deliver products or services with high margins: **Rating +.** The field currently has few suppliers and margins are high. Company has continued to add services to raise margins.
4. Provide customer satisfaction: **Rating =.** Company is able to deliver a service that meets customers' expectations.
5. Maintaining market position: **Rating =.** Company has a leading edge position currently, but it expects stiff competition as the market starts to expand.
6. Funding the business: **Ratings ?.** Company has been able to generate the funding it needs to put in large servers for bigger accounts as investors are worried about competitors that are starting to enter the market.

Birch Telecom, Inc.

Business Description: Provides phone, Internet, and data storage and retrieval services to 130,000 small business customers in more than 50 metropolitan areas in 12 states. Company filed for Chapter 1 bankruptcy protection in August 2005.

G–No
E–No
L–No

1. Acquire customers: **Rating = to ?.** Company has sales offices in each metropolitan area. Uses promotional mailings, trade show attendance, and cold calling.
2. Offer value to customers: **Rating ?.** Initially offered value when server costs were high and IT professionals hard to hire for a small to mid-sized company. With server costs coming down, and the growth of small consultant firms, value to customers has dropped.
3. Deliver products or services with high margins: **Rating ?.** Price pressures from larger companies entering the market and the lower costs of companies doing it all on their own have driven down margins.
4. Provide customer satisfaction: **Rating ?.** Customers are becoming more knowledgeable about doing it on their own and their willingness to pay more for a complete solution has dropped significantly.
5. Maintaining market position: **Rating ?.** The company is having trouble competing against both big firms and their target customers' do-it-themselves approach.

6. Funding the business: **Rating ?.** Additional funding is impossible after several years of declining sales and profits.

Product Oriented

Green Mountain Coffee

Business Description: Sells upscale coffee to convenience stores and businesses that are looking for a gourmet coffee to compete with Starbucks and other upscale coffee shops. Company promotes its green image, with a rigid environmental policy to help build brand recognition.

G–Yes	
E–Yes	
L–Yes	

1. Acquire customers: **Rating +.** Green Mountain changed from a small retail chain to selling wholesale in 1998. They were the only gourmet coffee marketer targeting convenience stores. Today they are known in the convenience store market and are a first choice when convenience stores face competition from coffee shops.
2. Offer value to customers: **Rating +.** Convenience stores need to compete against Starbucks as coffee purchasers typically buy two to three additional items. Green Mountain Coffee is one of a limited number of choices that convenience stores have.
3. Deliver products or services with high margins: **Rating +.** Coffee is a high-margin product, especially when it is shipped wholesale with only minor marketing costs.
4. Provide customer satisfaction: **Rating +.** Convenience stores are happy to be able to compete with the coffee chains and are happy Green Mountain Coffee is available to them.
5. Maintaining market position: **Rating =.** Currently competition is limited but that may change. Company recently signed a major agreement with Exxon/Mobil which may attract competition.
6. Funding the business: **Rating +.** Company's success and high margins allow it to easily raise any funding it might need for expansion.

Haige Manufacturing Company

Business Description: Produce self-propelled spraying systems primarily for growing hybrid corn. Products are sold direct to farmers rather than through a network of dealers. Company has been in business for 47 years and is well-known in the Midwest.

G–Yes	
E–No	
L–No	

1. Acquire customers: **Rating =.** Company has a well-known reputation and has many loyal customers. It does not, however, have the sales coverage a dealer network can offer, although the company compensates with a heavy show schedule that includes state and county fairs.
2. Offer value to customers: **Rating +.** Without a dealer markup the company has been able to offer more features than competitors for the same price.
3. Deliver products or services with high margins: **Rating +.** Direct sales generate higher margins than sales through dealers.
4. Provide customer satisfaction: **Rating ?.** Company can only provide strong service support in markets where it has service centers. Outside of those areas service is difficult for customers.
5. Maintaining market position: **Rating ?.** Dealers, many of whom have strong service departments, actively sell against Haige and, as small farmers disappear, it will have trouble holding onto market share.
6. Funding the business: **Rating ?.** Setting up a service network is expensive and difficult for Haige, but it is necessary to add centers to keep larger corporate-type farm owners happy.

Hayes Modem

Business Description: Hayes was one of the pioneering modem manufacturers for personal computers, producing the first modems in 1978. The company stayed in the traditional dial-up modem market but was unsuccessful entering the newer markets of remote access servers, high speed digital subscriber (DSL) lines, and cable modems.

G—No
E—No
L—No

1. Acquire customers. **Rating ?.** Customers are OEM computer manufacturers who are interested in very low pricing for dial-up networking modems.

> Original Equipment Manufacturer (OEM) is a producer that provides a product to its customers, who then proceed to modify or bundle it before distributing it to their customers. For example, if you supply an auto part to an auto manufacturer who then places it in a car for sale, you are an OEM supplier.

2. Offer value to customers: **Rating ?.** Dial-up modems are a mature technology where all competitors have similar margins.
3. Deliver products or services with high margins: **Rating ?.** Customers are buying from the lowest-priced supplier.

4. Provide customer satisfaction: **Rating ?.** Customers want low prices with special features.

5. Maintaining market position: **Rating ?.** Company is not competing in the new technology market for Internet connections.

6. Funding the business: **Rating ?.** Older technology doesn't attract the investors or loans needed to sustain the company.

Personal Service

Associated Speech and Language

Business Description: Speech therapists offer speech and occupational therapy to clients ranging from 2-year-olds to senior citizens. They have five clinics around the East St. Paul area.

G–Yes
E–Yes
L–Yes

1. Acquire customers: **Rating +.** Customers are referred by doctors and schools; parents and patients are very interested in improving their speech.

2. Offer value to customers: **Rating +.** Correcting speech problems providing an immediate enhancement of customers' quality of life.

3. Deliver products or services with high margins: **Rating +.** Parents of children with speech problems, or children of seniors with speech difficulties, are both willing to pay for results.

4. Provide customer satisfaction: **Rating +.** Clinics throughout the metro area make facilitated follow-up sessions when clients suffered setbacks.

5. Maintaining market position: **Rating +.** Company was the first one into the market and after two years still did not have a competitor.

6. Funding the business: **Rating +.** Company has been able to add a new clinic every year.

GameTrap–Turner Broadcasting

Business Description: Offers over 400 online games that consumers pick to play for $9.95 (down from $14.95 per month). Competes with AOL games, which is available online for free, plus several other sites. GameTrap offers a broad array of games to compete against AOL's established presence and strong community among game players.

G–No
E–No
L–Yes

1. Acquire customers: **Rating =.** Promotion and advertising to game players, word-of-mouth advertising, and two-week free trial programs.

2. Offer value to customers: **Rating = to ?.** GameTrap already dropped its prices once and it is unclear if it can establish value against AOL Games' free service.

3. Deliver products or services with high margins: **Rating = to ?.** Margins could be high if company can get enough users to justify systems costs.

4. Provide customer satisfaction: **Rating =.** Customer experience should be positive if customers feel the $9.95 per month fee is a good value.

5. Maintaining market position: **Ratings = to ?.** It is hard to hold its position until the company has signed up enough customers for it to be profitable. It is unclear at the moment whether or not that will happen.

6. Funding the business: **Rating +.** GameTrap is owned by Turner Broadcasting, which has deep pockets to fund losses for some time.

Atkins Diet Clinics

Business Description: Atkins Diet Clinics are retail stores that help people lose weight based upon the low carbohydrate Atkins Diet.

> G–Yes
> E–No
> L–No

1. Acquire customers: **Rating = to ?.** Relies on the popularity and recognition of the Atkins Diet in the public's eye. This was a big asset when the Atkins Diet was popular, but has turned south as publicity about the negative health effects of the Atkins Diet have grown.

2. Offer value to customers: **Rating = to ?.** Prices are consistent with other diet clinics, people do lose weight, but the overall health effects of Atkins Diet may be negative.

3. Deliver products or services with high margins: **Rating = to ?.** Profits are high when the diet plan has positive publicity and the Atkins approach is considered a top weight loss vehicle, but profits plummet when the Atkins Diet is under attack.

4. Provide customer satisfaction: **Rating =.** Customers do achieve significant short-term weight loss.

5. Maintaining market position: **Rating ?.** Company has been unable to hold market share in face of negative publicity.

6. Funding the business: **Rating ?.** Funding is difficult once the ship starts sinking.

Distribution Companies

Wholesale Marketer

Business Description: Company provides over 150,000 consumer products to Internet and eBay retailers who are looking for products to sell consumers. Primarily sells overstocks and secondary brands. Company's strength is that it can purchase major quantities at discount prices, and offers its vendors an easy way to sell lots of inventory and offer its customers access to small quantities of products at reasonable prices.

> G–No
> E–Yes
> L–Average

1. Acquire customers: **Rating = to ?.** Uses press releases, Internet, and Google advertising and promotion, and books, since Wholesale Marketer's CEO, Jeremy Hanks, is also the author of *eBay Inventory the Smart Way* (Amazon, March 2006). Drawback is that many of its customers buy only once and then go out of business.
2. Offer value to customers: **Rating +.** Offers pricing its customers can't otherwise obtain.
3. Deliver products or services with high margins: **Ratings +.** Purchasing large volumes of products and selling to very low-volume customers provides significant margins for the company.
4. Provide customer satisfaction: **Ratings ?.** Customers are satisfied with the product but in many cases their Internet marketing efforts fall far below their expectations, which can drive customers out of the business.
5. Maintaining market position: **Ratings = to ?.** A strong marketing campaign is required to continue to find new Internet entrepreneurs as others leave the market.
6. Funding the business: **Ratings +.** Margins have been strong enough to afford marketing and new product acquisition. Part of funding comes from collecting from customers prior to shipment and paying vendors in 60 to 75 days.

Harris Communications

Business Description: Supplies a wide range of products to dealers (310 at the last count) for deaf people including amplified telephones, baby cry signals, sign language dice, and pillow vibrating clocks.

> G–Average
> E–No
> L–No

1. Acquire customers: **Ratings =.** Trade shows, referrals from current dealers, Internet site, and e-mail promotions.
2. Offer value to customers: **Ratings =.** Provides an online menu of support services to help dealers make money and offers live support online to aid dealers on difficult sales.
3. Deliver products or services with high margins: **Ratings ?.** New Internet retailers have taken away customers and dropped the market's overall margins. Harris's major customers have become less important as consumers can find other outlets on the Internet.
4. Provide customer satisfaction: **Ratings = to ?.** Dealer customers need an edge to compete against online stores. Harris struggles to generate new ideas to keep dealers ahead of competition.
5. Maintaining market position: **Ratings ?.** Dealer customers' share of the market is declining and Harris's share of dealer business is dropping. To keep business, Harris needs a new community web site to attract consumers and direct them to dealers or it needs to go to an Internet-only business.
6. Funding the business: **Ratings = to ?.** Business is currently profitable but the margins and sales have been eroding and the only option available is self-funding.

Dyno Corp.

Business Description: Consumer products distributor specializing in skincare products from smaller manufacturers and selling them to drug store chains and mass merchants. Distributor has struggled as it has had trouble competing with pricing from major firms selling direct and because its brands lack strong name recognition.

G–Average
E–No
L–No

1. Acquire customers: **Rating =.** Large sales force, established market presence, trade shows, and advertising at key customers.
2. Offer value to customers: **Rating =.** Tries to offer new exotic, top-of-the-line products to keep getting shelf space. Strives to sign exclusive agreements with up-and-coming companies so it offers retailers unique choices.
3. Deliver products or services with high margins: **Rating = to ?.** Strong margins when it has market-distinctive products, but otherwise struggles.
4. Provide customer satisfaction: **Rating = to ?.** Must continue to find new, unique products in the marketplace for customers (retail stores) to keep offering it shelf space.

5. Maintaining market position: **Rating ?.** Becoming more difficult as major corporations (who don't use smaller distributors) expand their offerings and take more shelf space from smaller distributors.

6. Funding the business: **Rating = to ?.** Company has the financial ability to buy, or sign an exclusive license with new emerging firms.

Internet Company

365 Inc.

Business Description: Internet supplier of rugby and soccer merchandise. Company operates through 13 online retail stores selling both licensed and unlicensed merchandise along with two news-oriented sites (regarding rugby and soccer worldwide events).

G–Yes
E–Yes
L–Yes

1. Acquire customers: **Rating +.** Purchase key word search ads on search engines, promotions on other rugby and soccer news sites, but primarily generates customers by word of mouth due to its web presence since 1998.

2. Offer value to customers: **Rating +.** Diehard rugby and soccer fans and athletes can obtain products that are not otherwise easily available.

3. Deliver products or services with high margins: **Rating +.** Unique, highly desired merchandise by a fanatical customer base allows high-margin pricing.

4. Provide customer satisfaction: **Rating +.** 365's partnerships with key organizations allow the company to sell the quality licensed products its customers want.

5. Maintaining market position: **Rating +.** Company's early market entry and number of web sites, including two news web sites, provide a significant barrier for entry by new competitors.

6. Funding the business: **Rating +.** Company has been able to self-fund all of its growth with Internet-generated profits.

HomeApplianceOnSale.com

Business Description: Company acts as a go-between for customers and retailers, offering full product information on appliances and then connecting consumers to retailers in their area. Site also has product specialists that help consumers find

G–Average
E–No
L–Yes

the product they want through instant messaging. Site produces profits from retailers and appliance manufacturers who promote their products on the site.

1. Acquire customers: **Rating = to ?.** Customers are the retailers and manufacturers who support the site. Company acquires customers through ads, trade show attendance, and sales representatives.
2. Offer value to customers: **Rating = to ?.** Depends on how many consumers the company can deliver to the site. It is unclear how many consumers will research products online since many retailers carry broad product lines.
3. Deliver products or services with high margins: **Rating =.** Margins will be high if the site attracts enough consumers, retailers, and manufacturers to the site to cover its substantial upfront operating costs. Otherwise margins will be low.
4. Provide customer satisfaction: **Rating =.** Customers expect a return on promotional dollars in line with other marketing expenses. Site needs to deliver large numbers of consumers for this to happen.
5. Maintaining market position: **Rating ?.** Market position here is defined as percent of people purchasing appliances that come to the site. Since consumers rarely purchase appliances, the company will need steady and heavy promotion to keep consumers coming to the site.
6. Funding the business: **Rating ?.** Company needs a strong (and expensive) site to attract consumers and retail and manufacturer customers. It also needs constant upgrades and promotions to keep the site attractive. Funding will be difficult without any proof the site will attract enough customers or advertisers.

Sell 2 All

Business Description: An eBay power selling company that acquires products either by buying from manufacturers, making arrangements with drop shippers, or selling on a consignment basis. After six years in business the company filed for bankruptcy in 2006.

G–Yes
E–No
L–No

1. Acquire customers: **Rating +.** eBay provides easy access to almost an unlimited number of customers on its auction site.
2. Offer value to customers: **Rating =.** Buying low and selling low provides strong value to customers, but on eBay the company had trouble offering better bargains than other eBay sellers.
3. Deliver products or services with high margins: **Rating ?.** Margins are

low both because of eBay competitors and because the company's vendors demand higher pricing as other eBay merchants compete for their products.

4. Provide customer satisfaction: **Rating =.** Carefully selecting and pricing products produces satisfied customers.

5. Maintaining market position: **Rating ?.** As products to sell become less available due to competition from other eBay marketers the company has found maintaining market position difficult.

6. Funding the business: **Rating ?.** Declining sales and margins in a fiercely competitive market have made it impossible to raise more money to sustain the company.

Section 1
Part Two

The GEL Factors:
How to Evaluate Your Business

Chapter 4

The GEL Factors: Predicting Success

After a wild ride through the dotcom to dotbomb era, venture funding, angel investors, and business loans are back to normal levels. Everyone has learned a few lessons along the way, the most important being that business fundamentals always count. Businesses are analyzed today based on business fundamentals including a strong management team, a profitable business model, and a well-thought-out business plan.

The GEL Factors

The three main characteristics for producing success are what I refer to as the GEL factors (see Figure 1-1).

1. Having **G**reat customers
2. Sales are relatively **E**asy to make
3. The business will have a **L**ong life

A business will make a lot of money for a long time if it possesses all three GEL factors. To determine whether or not a business has these three points you need to evaluate customers, products, distribution networks, technical support, new product development, and production.

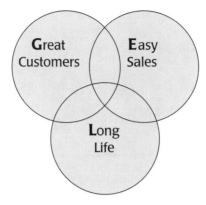

Figure 1-1. GEL: Overlapping Factors for Success

The GEL factor evaluation isn't a pass-fail test; it's to determine what's wrong with your business approach so you can repair it. Once you fine-tune your business so it delivers all the GEL factors, you will be able to write a great business plan.

How will you know if your business has these success points? That's what this first section of the book is all about—dissecting your business so you know you have great customers, easy sales, and long life. In reality, most new businesses won't have all the success elements in place at first. That's not a problem. This section will show you how to modify your business operation so it will really sizzle. Figure 1-2 details the analysis points of your GEL factor evaluation.

Starbucks—Brewing Success One Cup at a Time

Starbucks is a great example of a company with all the success factors. Its great customers are mid- to upper-income people who like to pamper themselves. There are a large number of those customers, they are easy to find by their neighborhoods and where they work, and they spend freely. Those customers provide plenty of value to the company because the dollar value of their sales is much higher than at traditional coffee shops, repeat business is great (like two to five times a week, and for some people two to three times a day), and the ongoing product support costs are very low as people consume the product.

G—Yes
E—Yes
L—Yes

Great Customers	Characteristics	Number Ease of Finding Spending Patterns
	Value to You	$ Value of Sale Repeat Sales Ongoing Sales Support
Easy Sales	Value to Customer	How Important Competitive Advantage Price/Value Relationship
	Customer Acquisition Cost	Entry Points Sales Support Required Promotional Activities
Long Life	Profit per Sale	Margins Up-Selling and Cross-Selling Selling Cost per Sale
	Investment Required	To Enter Business To Keep Market Share To Stay on the Cutting Edge

Figure 1-2. GEL Factors for a Successful Business

Starbucks also scores high in the easy sales criterion, starting with its value to its customers. The Starbucks "premium quality" image is important to its customers; its products are better than coffee from a coffee cart or a fast food chain; and its price, though higher than its competitors', is still a bargain for the "trendy and upscale" image their brand creates for its customers. In terms of acquiring customers, Starbucks started in Seattle, where it could afford the number of stores and the promotion it needed and its name recognition means it requires minimal ongoing promotional support.

As for long life, Starbucks meets all the profitability tests and has had little trouble holding onto its market share and expanding its store base. One advantage Starbucks had was a relatively low start-up cost. They only had two questions before opening. One was whether or not target customers would feel premium brands of coffee make them feel good about themselves, and second, how often those customers would come to Starbucks. Both of those questions could be answered at the test store that Starbucks opened in Seattle.

Kinkos—Tweaking the Concept

Kinkos started out as a copy center at major colleges and universities. To create recurring revenue it offered students copies of articles or papers that professors wanted to distribute to their classes. Kinkos would get a list of desired handouts from the professors, and then arrange for the rights to copy them and sell them to students. The idea was that Kinkos would have many products to sell to many students. As an additional service, Kinkos added computer workstations that students could use 24 hours a day.

G—No
E—No
L—Yes

This business approach had many elements for success. It provided a service professors wanted, it offered easy access to thousands of customers, and it produced a steady revenue stream.

There was just one problem: the work involved for each sale was too high. Kinkos needed just too many employees to execute its strategy for the fees students were willing to pay; the work was especially difficult when they made copies for just one class. This could have been the end of the story—except that Kinkos strategy of being open 24 hours a day had a side benefit: Kinkos started getting jobs for overnight production of copies of documents for businesses, plus other big orders like booklets for classes, presentations, court documents, legal documents for investors, and a whole range of other jobs that needed to be done at the last minute.

So Kinkos switched its business approach. It started locating its stores near large business centers, where there was always lots of last-minute rush business. All of a sudden Kinkos business model changed, focusing on businesses instead of students. The old model had students, who watched their money closely, as its target customers. The new model had as its target customers companies that would pay almost anything to get the rush job they needed done on time. Students thought a $20 purchase was big. Companies were happy spending hundreds and even thousands of dollars to get their documents done on time.

The results are clear. The new approach has a much better group of customers with critical needs that only Kinkos is addressing. The customers are easy to identify and happy to spend money to meet their needs. The new customer group is all it took to turn Kinkos into a profitable powerhouse.

Chapter 5

Finding a Great Customer Group

reat customers are probably the most important element for a highly profitable business. They allow companies to make strong profits and enjoy steady sales increases. Great customers aren't necessarily the customers with the most money, but they're the customers who value what you offer and are willing to pay for it. More importantly, they're the customers who will keep buying from you repeatedly and their purchases are significant

I DON'T MEAN TO IMPLY BY THE TITLE OF THE CHAPTER THAT THERE'S ONLY one right group of customers. All customer groups buy many products and there is a different right customer group for every product. These may sound like some pretty stiff requirements, but in fact many businesses are able to attract and keep a great group of customers.

Rockbottom Brewery is a restaurant chain that is growing fast around the country. It promotes Rockbottom Beer; has moderately priced food; and specializes in events, entertainment, pool tables, contests, and other once-a-month activities.

G–No
E–No
L–Yes

Why is Rockbotton different? Its average price per dinner is $15 to $20 per person, including a drink or two. At that price, many people are not only willing to visit the restaurant, but ready to visit it regularly. Plus

41

> ### Company Story—The Real Life
> ### Works Here but Not There
> Rainforest Café had a brief run of success in the late 90s in both high-traffic vacation or destination sites and upscale neighborhoods. At first the restaurants were all a success. But after a few years, Rainforest closed its restaurants that weren't at travel destination spots. What happened?
>
> Rainforest's target customer group is people who want to go to an upscale theme restaurant where the theme is more important than the food. At destinations, with a steady stream of new people, there were always enough customers. But away from destinations, people only occasionally wanted to visit a theme restaurant and there just weren't enough customers to keep buying its product.

Rockbottom always has something going on to appeal to the 20- to 35-year-old single crowd that frequently goes out for drinks and dinner.

In contrast, Rainforest's bill typically runs over $30 per person. That upscale price lowered the number of potential customers to the point that there just weren't enough to support the business at locations away from travel destinations.

G–Yes
E–Average
L–Yes

Six Key Factors for Evaluating Customers

		Desired	Excellent	Average	Poor
Customer Characteristics	Number	High			
	Ease of Finding	Easy			
	Spending Patterns	Prolific			
Customer Value to Company	$ Value of Sale	High			
	Repeat Sales	Many			
	Ongoing Sales Support	Low			

Figure 2-1. GEL Factor Customer Checklist

Number

Why It's Important

Businesses need a large enough customer base to cover their cost of running the business, meet income expectations, and have enough funds to keep sales momentum going with promotions and business expansions. Without a large enough potential customer group, you just won't have enough sales to cover these costs.

When It's a Key Concern

1. **Your product or service is inexpensive.** A low-priced product needs lots of customers to make money.
2. **Opportunities for repeat or add-on sales are limited.** If you need new customers every year, you need a big prospect pool.
3. **When customers can't find your business easily.** Customers look for some businesses in the Yellow Pages. If they don't look for your type of business, then you have to find them.
4. **People don't know about your type of product, business, or service.** They won't be looking for you if they don't know you exist.

Success Tip

Once you tightly define your customer group, check to be sure that there are successful businesses that appear to be targeting the same customer group. List what is similar about what the companies are offering and what is different. Pay particular attention to the price, the amount of repeat business, and the importance of the product to the customer. Be wary of customer groups that don't support successful businesses.

What Can Compensate

1. **You can present a compelling reason to buy.** You can get by with fewer prospects if your concept significantly meets a major customer desire.
2. **You can have a devoted distribution channel.** For example, people who buy map-related products are a small, widely scattered group of customers who go out of their way to find the few map stores that are in their area.
3. **You can be in places where your customers go.** A store that wants to sell ceramic tiles for home address numbers or garden plaques, for example, might thrive if located in a mall or town with a concentration of artisan stores and shops.

4. **You can be part of a network of organizations serving the same customer group.** You can promote effectively if you combine your efforts with other companies serving the market.

Ease of Finding

Why It's Important

You need to either easily locate customers or be easy for them to locate you. If it's hard to find customers, you may need to spend, spend, spend to find them and that cost might prohibit your success. For example, how does a company that sells small, in-home soda dispensers, similar to the ones in fast-food restaurants, find customers when only a small number of people will want the hassles of an in-home carbonated soda machine? Who are they and how can you find them?

When It's a Key Concern

Anytime that you can't depend on the following means of finding customers easily:

1. **Customers belong to clubs or associations related to your product.**
2. **There are trade or consumer magazines targeted at your customer group.**
3. **Customers can be identified through purchased lists.**
4. **Big events or trade shows target your customer group.**
5. **A distribution market serves your market.** Special woodworking shops or wild bird catalogs, for example, are targeted at customers who would otherwise be hard to find.
6. **Customers know where to look for you.** For example, people looking to go hunting in Montana look for lodges on the Internet or in hunting magazines.

Buzzwords

To be considered a *customer group*, people need to act in a similar manner. For example, people who cook dinner after eight hours of work are not a customer group. They'll behave differently depending on whether they have children, how many people they cook for, and whether or not they use prepared foods. A customer group would be working people who minimize their use of prepared food and are concerned about nutrition.

What Can Compensate

1. **Consolidate several products or services into a high-dollar purchase** that will justify spending lots of money to locate a few customers.
2. **Find potential customers through current customers.** A painter specializing in high-appeal party rooms knows that one person who loves to entertain knows many others who like to do the same, which can lead to referral business.
3. **Create a joint marketing campaign with other companies serving the same target group facing the same problem of finding customers.**
4. **Offer classes or seminars or attend trade shows to attract prospects.** A company that offers services to convert lawns into natural wildlife gardens might offer classes and demonstrations or start a club for people interested in a yard with natural fauna.

Success Tip

Confused customers never buy. Customers don't think the same way a salesperson does. Salespeople sell their product features, while customers worry about how a product will solve their problems or meet their desires. You'll always sell more if you gear your sales and marketing efforts toward showing the customers how they will meet their goals with your product.

Spending Patterns

Why It's Important

Some customer groups buy primarily on emotion and they will spend freely. Parents of young children may spend on impulse. Companies that want to be perceived as being leading-edge typically will spend money to protect their image. How customers spend impacts a company in two ways. The first is that customers who spend freely typically require less sales effort and customer service than customers who watch their money closely. The second is that customers who spend freely will often make bigger purchases, which simply results in more sales for less effort.

When It's a Key

1. **The sale is based on practical considerations rather than an emotional response.** People will almost always spend freely when it's an emotional purchase, such as a car, but they're always looking to cut costs for practical purchases.

2. **The product is not a priority purchase for the customer.** Customers who are reluctant will still always buy if it's a high priority for them.

3. **You don't have the resources to provide an intensive sales effort.** You can't shortchange the sales effort unless the customer is spending freely.

4. **The product needs to be purchased only once.** Unless your product is consumed and frequently purchased, you can afford only a limited sales effort for each sale and a limited sales effort won't sell customers who watch every penny.

How to Compensate

1. **Find a way to translate your sale into an emotional purchase.** Subway did a great job with its promotion of the student who lost over 100 pounds eating low-fat Subway subs. Giving people an easy way to lose weight stirs up powerful emotions.

2. **Sell a complete solution.** Find out what the customers feel is their goal when they buy your products or services and add products or services to help the customers achieve their overall goal.

3. **Set sales policies to make the buying decision easy.** Thirty-day trials, guaranteed returns, leases, and monthly fees versus a straight purchase are all ways to make the purchase decision easier for the customer.

4. **Concentrate your efforts on big potential accounts.** Most salespeople will tell you it's just as much work to sell $5,000 to a small company as it is to sell $200,000 to a big company.

5. **Add a product or a service that your potential customer will look for.** For example, people don't know where to look for invention marketing services. A firm might add prototype services, which its customers do look for in their Yellow Pages.

Success Tip

When you're having trouble locating customers, ask yourself what characteristics of customers make them strong candidates to buy your product. For the soda machine distributor, the people most likely to buy might be mid- to high-income people with more than three kids or people who have lots of kids around, like coaches. Those are people whom the company could find and sell to, so it would have a chance to succeed.

Dollar Value of Sale

Why It's Important

A high-dollar sale automatically creates a high-value customer. That means that a company can afford to devote resources to the customer, knowing that the sale will result in a profit. A company that supplies fuel stations for compressed natural gas vehicles may have an average sale price of $750,000. It can afford the sales support the customer needs to make a buying decision. On the other hand, a $5,000 to $8,000 industrial sale, especially to a small business, can be a dangerous price point, because the price still requires extensive sales support, but the size of the sale doesn't produce the necessary profits.

When It's a Key

1. **Sales support is required.** Sales of complex or technical items require an extensive sales effort, as do sales that are important for a company's operation and sales for which the final buying decision involves many people.
2. **Products are customized for each customer.** A person installing rock gardens needs to plan, select the right materials, and offer plenty of hand-holding support.
3. **The sales cycle is long.** Most families spend a lot of time thinking and planning before deciding to go ahead with a major home redecorating project. Many business-to-business sales start with an assessment of the available products, a preliminary request for budget approval, and then a final analysis by many people before a product is purchased.
4. **There are many competitors.** Your closing rate will typically be lower if you have many competitors, which means that you will have to make a large number of sales calls for every order you receive.

Buzzword

Closing rate is a term that states the percentage of prospects who give you an order. A 5 percent closing rate means that 5 percent of the prospects buy. Try to determine which type of prospects has the best closing rate for you and then concentrate on them.

5. **There are few opportunities for follow-up sales.** People put up vinyl siding only once in the time they own a home. They might, in contrast, buy a new entertainment system every three to four years.

How to Compensate

1. **Sell a turnkey solution.** A product that is integrated into a system requires a great sales effort, because the customer has a lot to worry about: in the end he or she is responsible for making sure the system works. Sell a solution that will not make the customer worry.
2. **Get the customers to come to you.** An average sales call can cost a company anywhere from $200 to $800. You can minimize that cost by having customers come to your location. Demonstrations, trainings, special events, and plant tours are all ways to attract customers to your location.
3. **Create an independent sales network.** Independent sales agents receive a commission on what they sell. Typically, companies have only minimal upfront fees with sales agents.
4. **Add product lines.** One way to increase the dollar value of each sale is to add complementary products so you have more items to sell. You can add your own new products or start to sell products from other companies.

The Market Niche

For the last 20 years, marketing has been about the *market niche* or, as the venture capitalists call it today, the space a company operates in. I don't mean to suggest in this chapter that the focus on a market segment or customer group (otherwise known as a *niche*) is not important. The goal of a business is to provide value to a customer; it can do that best by focusing on one group. You'll have a much easier time making money if you have a lot of free-spending, easy-to-find customers than if you try scratching out a living from a few, hard-to-find, tightwad customers. That's the point of the GEL analysis—finding a way to operate that will create a profitable business.

Repeat Sales

Why It's Important

Regular repeat sales are where companies can find really big profits. The sales costs are low, product support costs are usually low, and typically customers buy a standard product for which manufacturing costs are low. Companies can spend lots of money to get customers who will buy repeatedly and they can spend money to develop a strong relationship with those customers.

When It's a Key

1. **The dollar value of each sale is small.** It's difficult to drive down the cost of sales. It costs money to create a customer file, check credit, and monitor results even if a customer just calls you out of the blue to order.
2. **Customer service costs are high.** Selling to large customers, selling a product that interfaces with many other products, and selling a product with a large number of variations all typically require extensive customer service support.
3. **The purchase is a low-priority decision for customers.** It's difficult to get customers to make a purchase decision that they feel is a low priority. But it can still be worth the trouble to get the sale if it's an item people purchase regularly, such as office supplies, maintenance supplies, or telephone service.
4. **You have a small sales staff.** Customers making a major one-time purchase will be wary of a small company, because they will worry about after-sales service. But they will be happy to buy items they purchase regularly from a smaller supplier.

How to Compensate

1. **Create a more important purchase decision.** Ask how you can turn this purchase into one that will have a meaningful impact on a customer. For example, painters who create a memorable faux finishing look for a home will obtain much more business than a painter offering a straight paint job.

Success Tip

Controlling sales and marketing is a key to a successful business model. If you sell through distributors, sales and marketing costs—which include advertising, trade shows, direct mail, and brochures—should be no more than 20 to 22 percent of your sales revenue. If you sell direct to consumers, keep your costs below 30 percent.

2. **Find complementary ways to add value.** For the most part, what customers want is "no worries." Try to figure out what concerns a customer has about your type of purchase and then add services that make the decision "hassle-free."
3. **Create a low-cost sales plan.** You can keep sales costs low by selling on the Internet, through catalogs, through distributors and manufacturers' sales agents, at trade shows, or through another company.

4. **Expand the target market to a larger area.** If you can't get enough repeat business from your current market, you might need to expand to a bigger market. The bigger your target market, the more likely you'll find more customers eager to buy and your sales costs will be lower.

5. **Focus on big buyers.** Every market has big buyers, customers whose sales volume might justify your sales costs. If they don't, you need to reevaluate your business model.

Ongoing Sales Support

Why It's Important

When you sell office supplies, you don't need to offer much ongoing product support, which means that you get to keep most or all of the profit from each sale. But if you offer a lawn service that fertilizes lawns, you'll need more support. People will call up and check on whether or not a treatment is safe for pets or ask what to do if it rains right after the lawn is fertilized. All of these services cost money, and sometimes support costs can eliminate all the profits from a sale. Customers can represent high value to the company when they require little or no support, even if the profit margin per sale is low. The reverse is also true. An apparently profitable customer can quickly become a profit drain if support costs are high.

Pitfalls to Avoid

Most new companies badly underestimate the follow-up support required for products and services. Manufacturers find that people don't understand the simplest instructions and they break products despite clear warnings. Service providers find that customers change their minds about what they want or ask for one change after another. Find out what your product support costs will be from someone already in the industry.

When It's a Key

1. **Customers are buying an expected result instead of a defined product or service.** When people buy a food processor, for example, it's because they expect it will prepare some great exotic meals. Customers will complain if those meals don't come, even if the food processor works perfectly.

2. **Customer satisfaction depends on the application.** This is a common problem in business-to-business markets where customers have different applications. Some of those applications are bound to not work as well

as others and that will create follow-up costs.

3. **The product is new and users aren't familiar with its operation.** People will typically have trouble with any new device. With established products, customers will accept problems with comments of "That's just the way a product works" or they'll be able to find someone who can help them use it.

4. **Products are customized to a customer's application.** You're offering a beta unit when you're selling a customized product or service. Beta units have tons of kinks that can be worked out only in the field, which requires tons of product support.

Buzzword

Beta sites, beta units, and *beta customers* are terms you hear all the time with new companies or products. They simply mean test sites or test units. Companies often put products and services out at beta sites for 6 to 12 months to make sure the products or services work. It's not uncommon for support on beta units to exceed 25 percent of the sales price.

5. **Products interface with a number of other products.** Computer hardware and software products have only now, after two decades, started to interrelate well with each other, and those interface problems created product support costs.

How to Compensate

1. **Design products so that use is intuitive and "idiot-proof."** Do you read manuals? Probably not. You expect products to be intuitive. Most people wait until a problem develops—and then call technical assistance.

2. **Manage customers' expectations.** To a large degree, the supplier sets customers' expectations. If your advertising, sales presentations, and brochures all promise the world's greatest product, that's what customers will expect.

Success Tip

To determine just what expectations your customers have, ask your last 15 customers why they decided to buy from you, and what their expectations were. If those expectations are overly high, you have a major problem to correct. This is especially important for service providers, because customers can't see or touch what you're offering before buying.

3. Choose your customers carefully. Some customers have expectations you can't meet. Others have applications where your performance is marginal. Still others require ongoing support you can't afford.

4. Offer training programs at your location. Bringing the customers to your location is proactive, offers value to your customers, and is cost-effective for you.

5. Sell through a network that can provide service. Many industries—including power tools, lawn equipment, motorcycles, and industrial compressors—sell through a network of dealers that provide the service customers need.

Great Customers Exist Everywhere

Company Vignettes

Note to readers: I'll be tracking three companies—Dr. Spock Co., O'Naturals, and Jawroski's Towing and Service—in Chapters 5 through 7 to see how they compare on each GEL factor. The one point to notice is that a business needs all of the GEL factors for success.

There are six comparison factors related to great customers:

1. Number
2. Ease of finding
3. Spending patterns
4. Dollar value per sale
5. Potential for repeat sales
6. Ongoing sales support required

Dr. Spock Co.

Dr. Spock Co. provides parents advice on child rearing based on the works of Dr. Spock.

Parents of babies, especially parents who are professionals and in their 30s, appeared to the founders to be the right customer group. Their goal is to become the number-one spot that parents come to for baby advice, relying on the company's books, web sites, and pamphlets.

Evaluation on the basis of customers

1. Customers are older parents (28 years old and up); they are numerous. **Rating +.**

2. They are easy to locate through birth records, parenting shows, parenting magazine subscriptions, and purchases at child-oriented stores. **Rating +.**

3. This customer group is willing to spend money, and probably lots of money, for their children. It is not clear that customers value the advice of someone whose popularity peak was over 25 years ago (Dr. Spock). **Rating =.**

4. The dollar value of each sale will be modest, probably $10 to $50, so the company may lose money on the first sale. **Rating ?.**

5. Repeat sales could be strong, as children have new challenges as they grow older. Babies also go through stages very quickly, making it reasonable that customers will order every few months. **Rating +.**

6. The cost of ongoing customer support will be low. Information doesn't require warranty work or follow-up calls to be sure everything is working well. **Rating +.**

O'Naturals

O'Naturals is a chain of fast-food restaurants in New England that serve natural, organic foods.

Does fast food have to mean *fat* food? Not at O'Naturals, which is looking to gain a small part of the $20 billion natural food market. Its target customers are in wealthy New England towns that are populated by busy, highly educated, upper-income families.

Evaluation on the basis of customers
1. Although the market for natural foods is large, the number of customers interested in a natural/organic restaurant is unclear, even in the carefully chosen market. **Rating =.**

2. People preferring natural organic food should be relatively easy to find through their interest in food co-ops, subscriptions in organic food magazines, and their trips to farmers' markets and other health food–oriented businesses. **Rating +.**

3. The target customers appear to be committed to health foods and they spend extra money for their food of choice. But they are also probably willing to take extra time to prepare food themselves. **Rating =.**

4. The dollar sale value and profit per sale are modest, with a sale value of less than $7 per meal. **Rating ?.**

5. The number of repeat sales should be high, since O'Naturals is one of few natural-food restaurants and the only fast-food option for most of

its customers. If customers like the food, they should keep coming back. **Rating +.**

6. The ongoing customer support element of a restaurant is average. There's no sales follow-up required, but O'Naturals must ensure a pleasant dining experience, from good service to a clean restaurant, to keep customers happy. **Rating =.**

Jawroski's Towing and Repair

Jawroski's is a car repair and towing business in a fast-growing suburban area.

This business generates 25 percent of its revenue from towing, 40 percent from fleet repairs, and 35 percent from consumer drive-in traffic. The business does about $1.3 million per year in revenue and has been growing at a rate of 25 percent a year, with the growth of neighborhoods and businesses in the area. Most of Jawroski's towing business comes from vehicles that have broken down on a local major freeway.

Evaluation on the basis of customers

1. Almost everyone over the age of 18 has at least one car and many businesses have sizeable fleets. **Rating +.**

2. Customers couldn't be easier to locate. People who need a tow go looking for a business to help them. The businesses with vehicle fleets can be found easily through county and state business records, and almost every home has a car. **Rating +.**

3. People need their cars and they will pay to have them towed and repaired. They may not always appreciate their car repair services, but they definitely have to purchase the service when their vehicle needs it. **Rating +.**

4. Car repairs rarely run under $100, and towing costs of $75 to $100 are common. These are substantial sales, which means the company needs only a small number of sales each day. **Rating +.**

5. Repeat sales should be good if Jawroski's delivers quality service. Many people go way out of their way to go to a car repair shop where they've always gotten good service. **Rating +.**

6. Car repair shops don't have to work that hard to retain customers because people are leery of new shops. Car repair shops will keep their business as long as the shops give good service and keep current with technology changes. **Rating +.**

Many Ways to Skin a Cat

You've got stiff competition? Lucky for you there are still many methods you can use to build up a steady stream of business. I've listed here just a few of the tactics you can use.

1. Make part of your business a consumable product that clients have to buy repeatedly. Salt for water softeners, printer cartridges, and water for office coolers are all strong, consumable products.

2. Provide ongoing service. A lawn sprinkler system needs to be serviced in both spring and fall. Equipment suppliers to businesses frequently provide service contracts, both to produce ongoing revenue and to have the best chance of acquiring future business.

3. Sell a service rather than a product. Application service providers (ASPs) provide server-to-host software for their customers for a monthly fee, rather than selling software.

4. Spread your cost on a monthly basis, rather than requiring a major purchase. Leases, service contracts, and maintenance agreements all spread costs out over time. Customers are less likely to look for a new supplier if payments are low.

5. Provide incentives for increased use. Airlines do this with frequent flyer miles, as do grocery stores that give customers extra incentives when they reach certain purchasing milestones. For companies selling consumable industrial products, a popular tactic is to increase discounts for ongoing purchases.

6. Provide guaranteed trade-in value for upgrades. Allow companies to upgrade your products for a fee and give you a trade-in for current products. This is especially effective in software and fast-changing technologies.

Chapter 6

Making the Easy Sale

F or almost everything they buy, your customers can choose from many products or services. Entrepreneurs understand this and realize that they have to have better value than their competition. But another fact often overlooked is that prospects buy only a small percentage of the products they could buy. You need to do more than just deliver better value than your competitors; you need to deliver better value than other companies supplying radically different products.

For example, an average worker looking for a way to relax might enjoy golf, fishing, boating, camping, resort vacations, hunting, or gambling. People don't have time to pursue all these activities and, to a large degree, the value they perceive for each activity will determine where they spend their money.

E NTREPRENEURS HAVE TWO PROBLEMS TO OVERCOME IF THEY WANT truly easy sales. First, they need to offer something that customers really want to select among literally thousands of choices. Two, they need a cost-effective method of finding and communicating with those customers.

Company Story—Only One Winning Choice?

The battle was on for online research for academic papers and business papers. Originally it was a battle for college students, but students look for free downloads rather than ones they have to pay for. So, with the wrong target customer, both competitors changed course to succeed. Questia (*www.questia.com*) has 50,000 primary textbooks and 4,000 journal articles online and charges $19.95 a month or $99.95 per year for access to articles and books on its web site. Though it is a service for college students as well, the company mostly sells its service to businesses. Ebrary (*www.ebrary.com*) also started with college students and offered over 17,000 books online with searches free, but copying documents cost from 15 to 25 cents per page. Ebrary's original concept didn't last, as it couldn't generate enough money with its approach, and now it sells services to libraries, with over 900 current customers. What made their new approaches work while both companies' original model failed? They found customers who not only need their service (students also needed the service) but also they needed to be willing to pay for it (which is where selling to students failed). Both companies found a way to turn their failing model around into a profitable model that could sustain a business.

G—Yes
E—Yes
L—Yes

Six Key Factors for Evaluating Easy Sales

		Desired	Excellent	Average	Poor
Value to Customer	How Important	Important			
	Competitive Advantage	High			
	Price/Value Relationship	Low			
Customer Acquisition Cost	Entry Points	Many			
	Sales Support Required	Little			
	Promotional Activities	Low			

Figure 6-1. GEL Factor Easy Sales Checklist

Are You Important to Customers?

Why It's Important

Customers determine value by their standards and not by yours. Those standards have been evolving over the last few years to be more emotional than practical. Think of some of the great recent sales successes—Apple's iPod, Netflix, virtually all scrapbook products, and the restaurant chain Noodles. None of these offered a product or service that was truly important for customers. But customers wanted them because those items made them feel better. It was a reward for them; it said to others that they were important; it was to have fun; and it was to reinforce their own image of being a part of the smart crowd.

*T*he marketing reality is that buying is dominated by what buyers feel are their top priorities.

Companies operate in the same way. They want to project a variety of images that could include being a "breakthrough company," "marketing-driven company," "quality-conscious company," and even "cost-conscious company." Businesses need to project an image to their employees, vendors, customers, and competitors, and the image they desire is important.

The marketing reality is that buying is dominated by what buyers feel are their top priorities. People may have only two or three priorities that they can worry about and those are the only ones that drive their buying decisions.

When It's a Key Concern

1. **When the product is sold through a distribution network.** If the product is important to customers, then brand loyalty will probably exist, and distributors will buy products that have a loyal customer base. New companies will have trouble breaking into the market when customers are brand loyal because they won't switch if the product is important to them.
2. **Practicality is more influential on the customer's buying decision than fun or emotion.** Customers with money in their pocket are willing to buy from anyone's products that add fun, but they stick with the tried and true when it is a practical purchase.
3. **Customers aren't confident of the purchasing process.** Confused buyers rarely buy. And confused buyers take the trouble to learn about a product or service only if the benefit is very important to them.
4. **Purchases can easily be delayed or postponed.** For example, most of the time a new CD player isn't a necessary purchase; people can take a long time before deciding to buy. You'll waste time chasing customers who

keep delaying their purchase decision because the purchase isn't important to them.

5. **You have a limited number of contacts with any one customer.** You may get only one or two times to truly talk to a customer, and you need to be to selling something important to the customer if you want the customer to buy quickly.

How to Compensate

1. **Add an emotional context to the purchase decision.** Purchasing a new set of car tires is a practical decision. But Michelin added an emotional context to that decision when it showed a baby in its ads and promotions with the tag line "there's a lot riding on your tires."

2. **Create strong promotional programs to encourage immediate buying.** When your product or service isn't important by itself, you can often create a buying decision by making the buyer feel they will miss out if they don't buy right away.

3. **Use testimonials from industry experts or affiliations with other people trusted by customers.** Customers, both consumer and industrial, like to buy winning products, so testimonials can be a big asset.

4. **Target a segment of your customer group where your product or service is most important** rather than trying to sell to the broad market.

3. High use of consultants and other services to deal with the issue
4. Heavy news coverage and stories
5. Buyers buying. People started buying bigger homes and SUVs and the market responded.
6. Success in other markets. A retail concept might take off in one area and then spread, such as Staples, starting on the East Coast and then moving into the Midwest.

Your Competitive Advantage

Why It's Important

Customers have options—they can almost always find another product to meet the same need as your product. If you're going to succeed, you must have a strong reason for people to buy your product or service over competing products or services. The following is a list of some of the areas where you can get a competitive advantage.

1. Better support of customers' self-image
2. Best performance
3. More complete solution
4. Top perceived value
5. First with the newest technology
6. Most visual appeal
7. Highest-quality product
8. Best-known product brand
9. Lowest pricing

When It's a Key Concern

1. **A distribution channel is involved in the product.** Distribution channels are more knowledgeable about the differences among products and they evaluate all of the product choices. They will evaluate your competitive advantage and won't buy if they feel your advantage is not strong enough.
2. **Competitors are established in the market.** Buyers feel more comfortable buying from companies they know. With established competitors, a strong advantage is the only way to get noticed.
3. **You have fewer resources than competitors.** Companies that can't compete with a marketing budget must rely on their product differentiation to sell products.
4. **Customers can quickly tell which product or service is best.** For exam-

Pitfalls to Avoid

One sure way to guarantee problems in selling your product is to offer the same benefits as everyone else. How many companies targeting businesses have as their primary benefit that they help customers save money? Thousands. Customers quickly learn to avoid messages when they've heard them before.

ple, you can just try out two scanners and see that one has better resolution than another.

5. **Buyers are willing to shop for the best product.** Some people visit 10 to 15 furniture stores before buying a sofa. They check out all the product features before buying.

How to Compensate

1. **Add features and/or form partnerships.** A competitive advantage is one tactic for getting buyers to notice you. Another option is to join forces with a partner to either sell a package of products or services together to offer a more complete solution to the customers.

2. **Focus more clearly on a smaller target customer group.** Try to look for customers where your product has distinct advantages and then focus on that group.

3. **Offer convincing proof.** You might do this with test results, testimonials, documented cost savings, or customer evaluations of competing products.

4. **Increase your use of visual images.** People are heavily influenced by first impressions, and the visual is a key to that first impression. Having the best-looking package or the best-looking product is a big advantage.

5. **Become a market focal point.** You can sponsor events, conduct classes, be a leader of association committees, or sponsor a trade show or special speaker.

Perceived Price/Value

Why It's Important

People have a strong sense of what something is worth to them, a value that is determined by their own criteria. If a family takes a vacation to Disney World and the total bill comes to $5,000, will they consider that a great value? Some people will consider it a bargain because of Disney World's atmosphere and excitement, while others will resent the high prices and think that they would have been better off taking a camping trip to the mountains for $500. When you consider the perceived value of your product or service, it doesn't matter what the product or service costs to provide or what value you feel it has. It only matters what the target customer perceives the value of your product or service to be.

Buzzword

Value-added is a phrase you'll hear both from bankers and venture capitalists. It refers to services or add-ons that make a product or a service more valuable to customers. Putting a spring on the bows of kids' glasses is a value-added feature, because it makes it more difficult for kids to break their glasses.

When It's a Key Concern

1. **Customers consider the product or service a discretionary purchase.** I see flowers all the time at downtown outdoor malls. I buy some for my wife when I think the price/value is right.
2. **There are many other options for purchasing.** You won't buy a CD if you think the price is too high, because you have both many other places to buy a CD and many other CDs you could buy instead.
3. **Your product isn't well-known or is unproven.** People will take a chance on buying a new product if they feel it's a better value than current products, but they won't try a new product if they feel it's overpriced.
4. **Your customers are cost-conscious or value-oriented.** Engineers, accountants, and thrifty people all evaluate their product choices closely.

Pitfall to Avoid

When establishing the perceived value for your product, don't ask people what they feel it is worth or what they would pay. Customers almost always state an amount that's much lower than what they actually will pay. Instead, have your customers rank your product or service along with five or six other similar products or services by value. Your perceived value will be close to the products ranked just above and just below your product.

How to Compensate

1. **Add high value elements or services.** Better-quality components, stainless steel versus plastic, or an enhanced atmosphere for a store will raise perceived value.
2. **Drop features or benefits for which the perceived value is low.**
3. **Find a cheaper way to produce your product or service.** If you can't add enough value, you may be able to cut your costs so that your perceived value is acceptable to customers.
4. **Totally overhaul your business approach.** You may not be providing enough value to your customers. Successful businesses frequently change their business concept three to four times before finding something that works.

Entry Points Available

Why It's Important

How many ways can people start to buy from you? Those are your entry points. The more entry points you have, the easier it will be for you to find and sell to customers.

Here's an example: A copier supplier could just sell or lease a product. That's two entry points. The supplier could also offer a 60-day trial or offer the product for rent. That's two more entry points. The company could also have a web site and offer its product through an office supply store as an incentive for buying a year-long office supplies contract.

Entry points apply to all businesses. For a manufacturer of consumer products, entry points include anywhere a person can buy the product from stores, catalogs, and Internet sites. For a retailer, the entry points include how people can access the stores: the number of doors, the foot traffic by the store caused by nearby retailers, and the number of people who drive by.

When It's a Key Concern

1. **Your market is highly competitive.** Often the company that makes the sale is the one that makes its product most available with a high number of entry points.
2. **Customers may elect not to buy your product or service.** Life insurance, water filtration systems, or special phone headsets are all products people can elect not to buy. You have the best chance of encouraging a buy-

ing decision by having the product available in many locations and in many different ways.

3. **The sale is to a customer that provides limited revenue opportunities.** These customers don't justify sales and marketing expenses, and your best chance of success of a sale is having your product available in many locations.

4. **People have a short buying process.** For example, if I'm going to buy a fishing rod, I wait until I'm getting ready to go fishing and then I buy one at the first store I come to.

How to Compensate

1. **Go into the customer's world.** You need to hold contests, host seminars, be active in associations, and, in effect, go where customers go.

2. **Form partnerships and alliances to expand your market presence.**

3. **Create a strong prospect follow-up program.** If your customers can't easily run across your products, you can stay after them. Contact management programs like Act or Goldmine help companies set up programs for periodic mailings and follow-up phone calls.

4. **Create an easy-to-sell entry point.** CD- and movie-buying clubs have just two entry points: customers can respond to a direct mail piece and join through the Internet. Those entry points are easy for the customer to use.

Sales Support Required

Why It's Important

A new home, a piece of production equipment, an annuity, and a new, enterprise-wide software package are the types of buying decisions that people make only after extensive sales support, which includes presentations, demonstrations, training, help with installation, and answering repeated calls.

Sales support presents two problems for companies. The first is that it requires a big and expensive sales organization. This cost is overhead and, especially for start-ups, it can represent an expense that can produce substantial deficits for the first year or two. The second reason is that sales support costs can end up being 25 to 40 percent of revenue: that expense can take a heavy toll on the bottom line.

When It's a Key Concern

1. **When you have a complex or unknown product.** You need to worry about support anytime the customer needs help making a buying decision.
2. **The sales dollars you can generate from each customer are low.** To succeed, the sales support must be limited based on your profit per sale.
3. **Your resources are limited.** Sales support costs money, sometimes lots of money, in terms of sales staff, demo products, sales materials, and training.
4. **Your customers are widely scattered.** Complex sales requiring lots of sales support sometimes also require multiple sales calls, which are especially costly when customers are scattered.
5. **The purchase is not a high priority for the customer.** Customers tend to put off complex sales; this tendency is even stronger when the purchase is not one of the top two to three priorities for the customers.

How to Compensate

1. **Take responsibility for the complete solution.** Guaranteeing a result that meets the customer's expectations minimizes the need for sales support.
2. **Offer a service rather than a purchase plan.** No worries—that's what the customer wants when a purchase is complex, confusing, or difficult. Instead of just selling a product that the customer needs to figure out how to use, you can also provide a service that does the job for the customer.
3. **Set up or use a distribution network.** One of the advantages of distribution networks is that they have more frequent contact with your customer than you do and they can offer sales support at a lower cost.

Pitfall to Avoid

Many companies take it for granted that distributors will push your product once they decide to sell it. That's simply not true. One of the reasons that distributors can build customer loyalty is that they are careful to only present customers with products or services in which they have confidence. When using distributors, be sure you take the time to train them so they will push your product aggressively.

4. **Offer high sales compensation.** If you have a tough sale, you need the best salespeople, and you can get them only with generous compensation. Look for experienced salespeople with a history of high earnings.
5. **Enlist the aid of industry experts as part of your marketing team.** They can overcome customer confusion, skepticism, and worry—the big three reasons that a sale becomes difficult.

Promotional Activities Required

Why It's Important

Promotional activities are another item that can be a prohibitive expense. Retail stores in offbeat locations can spend money on big events, advertising, attendance at trade shows, or direct-mail campaigns. Other stores will pay the expensive rent of a mall to bring in customers. On the other hand, some businesses have low promotional expenses; some can operate out of homes and simply call on the four big customers in their area. A group of ex-Lockheed engineers, for example, started a product design business with just one customer, Lockheed. They had no promotional budget. High promotion costs result in more overhead, higher prices, and generally a riskier business concept.

When It's a Key Concern

1. **Customers are difficult to locate.** You need to promote aggressively when you can't buy a list of customers, don't have events where customers gather, or can't team up with other suppliers serving the same market.
2. **You can't be sure when a customer is going to buy.** Which business this year will be buying new office partitions for an employee expansion? You can spend lots of money when you don't know which customers to concentrate on.

3. **Low to moderate pricing and average sale value.** The more customers to whom you need to promote your product or service in order to generate a profitable sales level, the more you need to be concerned about promotion expense.

4. **You need to create a new brand or product against established competition.** Getting brand recognition takes a long time, especially if competitors have an entrenched customer base.

5. **You have a new category of product or service.** The toughest job of promotion is when people aren't even aware that your brand or service is available.

How to Compensate

1. **Establish a recurring revenue stream from each customer.** A monthly service produces more sales than a one-time product sale.

2. **Add new products or services that customers need.** Many companies have their own product line but are also distributors for other manufacturers. Companies will also be sales agents for other companies.

3. **Develop tools to attract customer interest early in their buying process.** Classes, seminars, and informational web sites are all ways to find customers well before they're ready to buy.

4. **Create extremely effective promotional materials or visual images.** We live in a visual age, and I've found that people are four to five times more likely to remember your product or service if you associate a powerful visual image with it.

Success Tip

The best visual images don't focus on your product, but instead on the solution or result for the customer. This helps customers relate the product to their situations. A picture of a kitchen cabinet doesn't connect with a customer, but a glistening remodeled kitchen does. Your visuals should reflect the result customers want when they buy your product.

5. **Have a distinctive product or service feature that makes your company memorable.** You can cut significantly the number of exposures customers need before buying if you have one unique, dramatic feature or benefit.

Easy Sales Are Hard to Come By

Company Vignettes

There are six comparison factors related to easy sales:

1. How important the purchase is to customers
2. How strong your competitive advantage is
3. How customers perceive your price/value relationship
4. How many sales entry points you have
5. How much sales support is required
6. How many promotional activities you'll need

Dr. Spock Co.

Dr. Spock Co. provides parents with advice on child rearing based on the works of Dr. Spock.

The entire premise behind Dr. Spock Co. is that raising children is extremely important to a certain segment of professional parents. That importance is the motivator that drives the business.

Evaluation on the basis of easy sales:

1. Children are important to all parents and bringing up children well is important to a large segment of professional parents of infants. **Rating +**.
2. Customers' perception of Dr. Spock's competitive advantage over newer authority sources is unclear. **Rating ?**.
3. Customers may not see Dr. Spock as having a strong price/value relationship unless they first value Dr. Spock's advice. **Rating ?**.
4. The company should be able to have a large number of entry points, especially if they get their pamphlets distributed by doctors. **Rating +**.
5. Sales support of users will be low because of Dr. Spock's name recognition to certain customers and because the purchase price is relatively low. **Rating +**.
6. Promotional activities will be needed, especially as the customer base will change each year, but the promotional activities will still be low due to brand name recognition of its targeted customers. **Rating +**.

O'Naturals

O'Naturals is a chain of fast-food restaurants in New England that serve natural, organic foods.

O'Naturals founders developed a stronger position for customer value because they started with what they felt was an unmet customer need: healthy fast food. O'Naturals has to deal with two aspects regarding customer value. The first is whether healthy food is important to O'Naturals' customers. The answer is clearly yes. The second is whether or not fast food is important to people who want healthy meals. The jury is certainly out on this second point.

Evaluation on the basis of easy sales:

1. In terms of importance to the customers, healthy food alone rates a +, but healthy fast food is at best an even choice. **Rating =.**
2. O'Naturals clearly has a competitive advantage over other fast-food restaurants and an advantage in terms of speed over other healthy food restaurants or eating at home. **Rating +.**
3. The customers' view of the O'Naturals price/value relationship depends on how much they value service speed. People willing to take the time to eat healthy food may not place a premium on saving 15 minutes a day at a fast-food restaurant. **Rating =.**
4. O'Naturals has only a few restaurants and the number of entrees they can offer will be limited because they're a fast-food restaurant. **Rating ?.**
5. Sales support will be important for O'Naturals as it will need to reinforce on each customer visit that it's serving healthy food. The positive point for O'Naturals is that it should be inexpensive to offer that support, with placards on the table and information in the restaurant. **Rating +.**
6. Promotional activities will be expensive for O'Naturals. While word-of-mouth advertising might work for dedicated healthy eaters, promotion will probably be needed for people with only a mild interest in healthy foods. **Rating ?.**

Jawroski's Towing and Repair

Jawroski's is a car repair and towing business in a fast-growing suburban area.

Jawroski's will be judged by how effectively the employees solve the customers' problems, the quality of their service, and how their price compares with the competitors. If they do well by those three criteria, customers will keep coming back and word-of-mouth advertising will carry the business.

Evaluation on the basis of easy sales:

1. Car repair is obviously important: if your car is not working, you need it fixed. **Rating +.**

2. Jawroski's has built its competitive advantage around its high-test equipment and its ability to repair cars right the first time. This is important to its fleet customers and people in its nearby upscale neighborhoods. All of Jawroski's competitors are smaller shops with less technology. **Rating +.**

3. Jawroski's customers value getting results above all else, so they perceive that Jawroski's has a strong price/value relationship. **Rating +.**

4. Jawroski's number of entry points is limited, but the company's ideal location on a busy street compensates. **Rating +.**

5. Jawroski's sales support is simply giving good service so that cars work. Jawroski's high-technology garage and the owner's commitment to keeping his employees well-trained give Jawroski's all the sales support it needs. **Rating +.**

6. Jawroski's depends on its location for promotion. But it can also generate low-cost promotions in the neighborhood by sponsoring sports teams, allowing high school organizations to hold car washes on its site, and doing inexpensive neighborhood mailings. **Rating +.**

The Buying Binge

ADC Telecommunications is one of the market leaders in fiber optic technologies for the telecommunications and computer industries. In the late 1990s and early 2000s, ADC purchased several companies that provided products that were complementary to its own. ADC was able to cut its cost of acquiring customers dramatically in several ways because of a bigger product line.

G—No
E—Average
L—Yes

1. Add entry points, especially in equipment markets. ADC's customers require many products to achieve a solution to their needs. By expanding its product line, ADC improved the chances that a customer would call for at least one product.

2. Cut sales support costs for each product line. Customers are looking for a complete integration solution. A broader product line allows ADC to consolidate its whole product line into its training and demonstration programs.

3. Make promotional programs more effective. The more complete your solution, the more your messages and promotional programs will interest potential customers.

Chapter 7

Building a Long Future

A LONG FUTURE DEPENDS ON MONEY: HOW MUCH YOU NEED TO invest, how much you make on every sale, and how much you need to stay in business. The most important factor is probably profits from every sale, but even profitable companies can be waylaid if they need too much investment. Even a business with a great concept can have unpredictable costs, such as an unexpected lawsuit, a sudden price increase from a key vendor, or high promotional expenses in response to an aggressive competitor. A business can also find itself faced with unexpected investments required to meet a competitive market. A business ideally set up for long life has margins high enough to absorb unexpected costs and requires just modest investments to adjust to market and competitive changes.

Company Story—Nothing Comes Easy

GiftCertificates.com had a simple business concept. It would be a Web site where people could easily buy gift certificates from a wide variety of retailers. The company set up 4,000 corporate clients and partnerships with 700 merchants, including major retailers like Bloomingdale's. The company had high upfront costs setting up, but

G—Yes
E—Yes
L—No

that was to be expected. The problem was having high margins in the face of competitive pressures and high ongoing investment to hold onto the business.

The first problem was smaller competitors offering the same package of services for lower prices. GiftCertificates.com responded by buying out two of the bigger competitors, GiftSpot.com and GiftPoint.com, acquisitions that brought the company's debt load up to $90 million. Next the company had to worry about big portal sites like AOL and Yahoo! Locking the big sites into GiftCertificates.com would be difficult when AOL and Yahoo! could offer the same service if GiftCertificates.com is successful. The company has responded by repeatedly going back to the market for additional capital to promote itself. But can GiftCertificates.com survive? Their only chance is to hold onto market share by heavy and repeated expenditures to buy off competitors, promote the site to potential customers, and keep its predominant position as an incentive gift supplier to 70 percent of the *Fortune* 500 companies.

Six Key Factors for Evaluating Long Life

		Desired	Excellent	Average	Poor
Profit per Sale	Margins	High			
	Up-Selling and Cross-Selling	Much			
	Ongoing Product Costs	Low			
Investment Required	To Enter Business	Low			
	To Keep Market Share	Low			
	To Stay on the Cutting Low Edge	Low			

Figure 7-1. GEL Factor Long Life Checklist

Healthy Margins

Why It's Important

Healthy margins with adequate sales are by far the number one indicator of a healthy company. When I started in business right out of college, I could never understand why finance people had so much power in a company.

After all, I thought, they don't do anything constructive. But I've since learned that I was wrong. Since companies often survive on a profit of 2 to 5 percent on sales, a few percentage points difference in margin can make all the difference in the world between making and losing money. Controlling margins is one of the most effective ways to determine just how successful a company will be.

When It's a Key Concern

1. **Healthy margins are always a key concern.** What about the old adage that we'll make up for a low margin with high volume? Baloney. Wal-Mart doesn't have low margins. They have low prices because they have the buying volume to drive down the prices they pay. The fact is that the strategy of low margins and high volume is a risky strategy. You incur large upfront costs to generate high volume, and if the demand shifts even slightly those high costs will be a huge anchor on your profitability.

How to Compensate

1. **Add more value.** Companies that match each other's pricing typically end up losing money. The better approach is to find out what customers really want and then provide that.
2. **Cut major costs.** A company with a sustainable advantage in costs is almost impossible to defeat.

Success Tip

Service companies and retail stores have costs that they should evaluate constantly. A maternity shop may decide to only keep one size of each garment on the floor with offsite warehousing to keep down inventory costs. Service companies may have high rent, which represents a cost problem, or they may have too many of their employees in administrative positions, raising their costs of doing business.

3. **Find another method of distribution.** Sometimes low margins are caused by distribution costs. For example, if you sell to a wholesaler that sells to a distributor that sells to a retailer you'll only be receiving a fraction of the final retail price. It's not always clear that one or more of these steps in the distribution chain is adding that much value in getting the products to customers.
4. **Choose another customer group.** You need to find someone who finds

more value in your products or service than your current customer group.

5. **Lower your overhead structure.** Overhead is a heavy burden for every company, and you need to check it periodically, whether it's rent, phone bills, or computer reports, to keep costs in line.

Up-Selling and Cross-Selling

Why It's Important

Building customer trust is time-consuming and expensive. Once you have it, each subsequent sale is easier to make than the previous sale. This is one of the main reasons that people use manufacturers' representatives and distributors. They have already built a bond with customers. Additional sales to an existing customer base are much easier to make than sales to new customers. Businesses that can cross-sell or up-sell have a much better chance of improving their profits per customer.

Buzzwords

Cross-sell refers to selling another type of product to the same customer. For example, a cross-sale for a retailer of upscale audio equipment might be big-screen TVs or a car audio system. An up-sale is adding features to an already existing purchase. A TV retailer, for example, would consider a "surround sound" stereo system to be an up-sell because it is an upgrade of a TV purchase.

When It's a Key Concern

1. **A purchase is rarely made.** People buy a refrigerator once every 10 years. An appliance store can make much more money if they can add significantly to the customer's purchase with an up-sell or cross-sell. The extra sale has to be made on the spot since the customer might not come back for another 10 years.

2. **The sales costs are high relative to the purchase price.** All products or services have a certain value to the customer that limits what you can charge. The amount might not cover your sales costs unless you can increase your profit by selling additional items to most customers.

3. **Future customer contact is unlikely.** When you call to order a product from a TV commercial you are unlikely to call that company again.

4. **The purchase is a low priority.** Customers are often responsive to an up-

sell or cross-sell when they are making what is for them a high priority purchase, but not when it is a low priority.

How to Compensate

1. **Add a consumable component to your sales mix.** Water softener manufacturers deliver salt and put it into water softeners. Software companies charge a monthly lease fee for software and others have a monthly maintenance fee. This will keep customers in constant contact with you, allowing more opportunities for up-selling or cross-selling.
2. **Sell private-label products.** Find products that complement yours or are a natural up-sell or cross-sell and then arrange to sell them under your name. This is especially effective if the private-label product is a consumable product.
3. **Combine ongoing with one-time services.** An air conditioning service company for industrial buildings might include yearly cleaning of the vents, shut-down and start-up services, and even air quality monitoring services.
4. **Restrict your sales to high-yield customers.** You can't afford to try and sell to every potential customer. Find the customers that you can sell to profitably and then just forget about the others.

Ongoing Product Costs

Why It's Important

A supplier of playground equipment to children's day care centers knows that his customers have steady turnover, and the supplier needs to expect numerous follow-up calls and inquiries over the life of the equipment. Garden shops know that trees it sold that die within 12 months will have to be replaced. Computer equipment manufacturers know that changes in computer hardware and software will necessitate follow-up support for their equipment. In every case, the supplier may need to provide service at no charge to the customer, but the service is certainly not free to the supplier. Too many ongoing costs per sale can certainly kill a company's profits.

When It's a Key Concern

1. **There is turnover among people using your product.** An advertising agency will have high costs if the main contact at its customers keeps changing. The agency will need to offer more personal contact, more

sales presentations, and more no-charge demonstration work to ensure they don't lose the account.

2. **Your product or service interfaces with many other products or services.** You may need to offer new connections, or you might need to integrate your equipment to new products offered by other manufacturers after the customer has already purchased your product.

3. **The market you compete in has rapid changes.** Changes in the market typically mean your customers may be using your product in different ways. They'll be contacting you for updates on how to use your products, and you may need to provide adjustments to the products or services you've provided.

4. **Customers don't have the knowledge to adjust for or correct small problems.** When something small goes wrong with a lawnmower most homeowners know how to fix it. Customers don't know what to do when unfamiliar with a product.

5. **Your product or service replaces a well-known product.** Established products typically have all of their kinks worked out and they run smoothly for customers. Customers expect a new product to work just as smoothly, which rarely happens with a new product.

How to Compensate

1. **Set your customers' expectations.** Don't act as if your product or service is "Drop and Run" (you sell it and never come back) if in fact you know the customer will need a fairly large amount of ongoing product support.

2. **Create online or ongoing training and service.** Let the customer know up front that you have ongoing training and service programs. Have the staff in place to execute those programs, and plan on these expenses in your budget and the price of your offering.

3. **Plan product upgrades that track industry changes.** Hewlett-Packard is a good example of a company that anticipates industry changes and has the product upgrades available right when their customers need them.

4. **Make accessibility to solutions easy for customers with problems.** Have solutions to problems prepared in advance that you can send to customers with problems. Many people will fix a problem themselves if you tell them how to do it.

Big Steps Often Work

One of the big problems many companies have when dealing with cost issues and particularly margin issues is that they think incrementally. That may work to tweak a business just a few margin points, but you should also consider big radical moves. I worked with a $30 million company that sold products to the dental industry. The company made money most years, but the profits were always modest. The company had a large administrative staff, big marketing and R&D departments, and three manufacturing plants.

Looking at the customer base the company found that about 40 percent of its customers were very loyal. The rest of the customer base had varying degrees of loyalties, but the last 20 percen, were not only not loyal, they were expensive to sell to as they required lots of product support. The company's strategy was to cut nonmanufacturing office personnel by 80 percent and just sell to its loyal and semi-loyal base. Sales dropped about 25 percent, but profits went up over 800 percent. Incremental thinking would never have come to this conclusion. Consider your business from all angles to find solutions to profitability problems.

Costs of Entering the Market

Why It's Important

Start-up costs include manufacturing costs, setting up the company, and launching a marketing and sales campaign. The main concern most people have is having enough money to launch the business. But from a GEL factor perspective it's not just how much money—after all, companies raise hundreds of millions of dollars in initial investments—it's how much money the investment will make. Ideally you want the annual market sales potential to be at least 10 times the amount of the investment required. Otherwise you have to question whether or not the investment is worth the risk of the business failing.

When It's a Key Concern

The amount of investment versus the market potential is always key, but in some cases it is of critical importance.

1. **You have an untested business concept.** New business concepts have plenty of kinks and a business's chance of success is in doubt if the upfront investment is high and you can't be sure when the business will turn a profit.
2. **The product life cycle is short.** A short product life cycle means that a company has to get its investment back in a big hurry, which can be hard to do with a big initial investment.
3. **You don't have access to significant resources.** You and your inner circle

---

Pitfall to Avoid

Too often new entrepreneurs assume that competitors will just keep on operating the way they always have even if they lose market share to the new entrepreneur. Unfortunately, competitors do respond, sometimes decisively, when a new entrepreneur takes business.

Businesses need a feature that gives them a sustainable advantage, one that competitors can't easily duplicate, in order to succeed.

---

of initial investors have to provide a significant share of the start-up capital. If you are low on funds, pick a project that only requires a modest upfront investment.
4. **You have a major competitor.** You'll need to provide twice as much service for the same price as the big competitor because customers are just as skeptical of newcomers as they are comfortable with a major supplier.

How to Compensate

1. **Partner up with major players.** Cut your investment by partnering with another company and using its resources. You might have a partner handle all of your administrative functions, use their sales force, or simply use the partner's name for credibility.
2. **Pre-sell contracts to major prospects.** You will reduce your risk if you convince three or four customers to sign a contract before you make the

initial investment. Distributors, retailers, and buyers will often place an order if you offer the right incentives and have an innovative product or service.

3. **Quickly corner a segment of the market.** With a big upfront investment you want to avoid a lengthy period waiting for sales. One tactic is to focus on a small part of the market to generate a solid, though small, sales base.

4. **Have an innovative promotional or sales strategy.** You can set up sales, distribution, or promotional programs to lock up customers, such as selling a product based on a monthly service charge rather than a standard sales price.

5. **Outsource high-cost operations.** Manufacturing, promotion, and staffing require the biggest upfront costs, and these functions can be outsourced to other companies. You can also share administrative costs and overhead expenses by sharing office space.

Costs to Hold Onto Market Share

Why It's Important

The company story box at the beginning of this chapter was about GiftCertificates.com. Buying market share for six months is great if the edge you generate will sustain itself afterward with a much lower promotional level. If it won't, the company will have trouble surviving. Buying market share with lower prices is typically a short-lived strategy because competitors will respond with their own low prices. The same is true with promotions and sales effort. The competitors can match you and then your only recourse is to try and outspend your rivals.

When It's a Key Concern

1. **Customers don't perceive differences between products.** Levi's held major market share in the jeans market for years with heavy promotion. Then their promotional efforts slowed down, and they immediately lost market share.

2. **Large, established competitors are already in the market.** Big companies have their own promotional war chest that you have to compete against to get noticed.

3. **Alternative low-cost marketing methods (events, shows, association and user groups) are not viable.** Customers have a keen interest in some

product categories, such as wedding dresses, or Internet marketing, and they will come to events and notice new market entrees. If you don't have the strong interest, you will need a strong promotional budget to hold market share.

Success Tip

Alternative marketing tactics work best when a product or service is new and unusual. You don't, however, have to have a radically new segment to use this tactic. Garden stores that offer classes in English rock gardens are offering a slight twist that will generate customer interest. Paint and home improvement stores are taking the same tack with faux finishing classes, merchandise, and displays.

4. **You can't gain an advantage with sales and/or distribution tactics to minimize promotional costs.** Offering the highest commissions, setting up franchises or distributorships, signing exclusive agreements with key distribution outlets, and signing up customers to long-term contracts are all options to minimize promotional expenses.
5. **Marketing and promotion costs are high.** Marketing to teenagers is expensive. Advertising on TV or in teen-oriented magazines costs lots of money as does sponsoring rock bands or other events.

How to Compensate

1. **Find more effective ways to differentiate your product.** Find one important desire of your customers and then create a feature or benefit that customers can easily notice.
2. **Compete only in segments where your product is differentiated.** Stop trying to sell to markets where your costs are high and competition stiff because prospects can't see your advantage.
3. **Form partnerships to offer a better customer solution.** Customers love to

Buzzwords

Features are the specific tasks or image your product or service offers. Benefits are why those features are important to the customer. An automatic transmission on a car is a feature. The benefit is that people don't have to shift gears manually. Benefits are more important than features, because customers actually buy a solution, which in this case is an easy-to-drive car. So think in terms of solutions rather than features when you are trying to differentiate your company from the competition.

buy a "plug and play" solution—something works immediately. Once you understand the solution the customer wants, you'll find that there are plenty of potential partners available.

4. **Go out of the box with your name and promotion strategy.** Companies now use billboards on vehicles that drive around to promote their business to reach customers more cost-effectively. Another popular tactic is street marketing teams that are sent to an event to promote a new product cost-effectively.

5. **Refocus on a smaller market segment that you can afford.** Companies have to be sure they get a return on the money they spend, and sometimes that means they have to go after a small market where their promotional efforts will have an impact.

Costs to Stay on the Cutting Edge

Why It's Important

Nothing succeeds like having the newest, best products and services that everyone wants. The demand for the product brings you the promotional recognition you need without having to pay for it. If you are not on the cutting edge, not only are you at a distinct disadvantage when selling every customer, but you also are faced with the need for a much higher promotional budget. Cell phones are a good example. When they first came out there were just a few competitors with state-of-the-art products, and those companies had very small promotional and advertising budgets. They didn't need to advertise because people knew about the products from magazines and newspaper stories. Today consumers don't differentiate cellular phones that well, and companies have to advertise heavily.

When It's a Key Concern

1. **Customers are gadget or new technology lovers.** These customers know what's happening in the market, and they won't stay with you even one week if someone else introduces the latest gadget.

2. **Customers rely on cutting-edge products for status.** Salespeople, business executives, and others always want the latest electronic gadget so they look like they are on the cutting edge.

3. **New technology significantly reduces costs or raises productivity.** This means customers will quickly switch to a new supplier with improved features in order to gain those savings.

4. **Current technology has well-known deficiencies.** Diesel truck technology has two big deficiencies: they are big-time polluters, and they have low gas mileage. Truck owners immediately look at new products that can minimize those problems, providing they have a minimal cost.

5. **Rapid product or service changes occur in the industry.** This applies to most markets today. The pace of product change and improvement has never been higher.

How to Compensate

1. **Become tightly affiliated with a segment of the target market.** You can't stay on the cutting edge of development if you don't have a great understanding of your customers' current and upcoming needs.

2. **Use a customer advisor group to keep ahead of the market trends.** Meeting with key customers or prospects three to four times a year will help you keep a firm grasp of what customers want.

Pitfalls to Avoid

Many executives feel they don't need customer input. That's true when a company knows:

1. What solution every customer wants.
2. The customer's priorities for each aspect of the solution.
3. All the upcoming changes from products or services the solution interacts with.
4. New and emerging trends in the customer's world that will impact their solution.

Nobody can know all this all the time. You need customer input.

3. **Use outside product design sources.** Some companies have a relationship with outside inventors. Explain to the outside sources, inventors, or product designers about your upcoming needs and offer to pay a royalty on any products they develop that are introduced.

4. **Focus spending on product development.** If the cutting edge is where your company belongs, you are often far better off spending your efforts developing new products or services than you are spending money setting up a well-oiled administrative staff.

Great Model Fundamentals Require Discipline

Company Vignettes

This time, we'll compare these factors:

1. The health of margins
2. The amount of up-selling and cross-selling available
3. The size of ongoing product support
4. The cost to enter the business
5. The cost to keep market share
6. The cost to stay on the cutting edge

Dr. Spock Co.

Dr. Spock Co. provides parents advice on child rearing based upon the works of Dr. Spock.

The publishing industry has large fixed costs in producing the first unit, and then low costs to produce more copies. The situation is much better in e-publishing where there are no upfront print costs. The nice point of Dr. Spock's concept is that while the upfront costs are high, future costs should be modest as the company should generate up-sells and cross-sells.

Evaluation of Dr. Spock's potential for long life:

1. Dr. Spock will have high margins for everything they sell once they overcome their upfront costs. **Rating +.**
2. People who adopt the Dr. Spock approach are likely to buy many products and services as their child goes through their early years. **Rating +.**
3. One nice aspect of the publishing costs is that there are few ongoing sales costs except returns. Many of Dr. Spock's products and services will be sold over the Internet where return costs will be low. **Rating +.**
4. The upfront investment is high but certainly justified based on the Dr. Spock brand name and the large potential market. **Rating +.**
5. Funding to hold market share, based on the company's evaluation of the acceptance of Dr. Spock, should be relatively low. **Rating +.**
6. Dr. Spock won't need to spend money to stay on the market edge as children and their needs don't change. The company's only significant spending, if they choose to do it, would be research showing that the Dr. Spock method is still relevant. **Rating +.**

O'Naturals

O'Naturals is a chain of fast-food restaurants in New England that serve natural organic foods. Many fast-food restaurants have struggled over the years because the profit per sale is low. After all, one of the dominating benefits of fast food is low prices. Restaurants depend on volume, and volume at every meal. Fast-food restaurants try cross-selling and up-selling with upsizing and desserts, but they only add modestly to sales. All three costs are a problem at fast-food chains as it is tough to compete with McDonalds.

Evaluation of O'Naturals potential for long life:

1. Margins at fast-food restaurants like O'Naturals are significantly lower than traditional restaurants. **Rating ?.**
2. Cross-selling at a restaurant is usually associated with selling more food, which is not likely with a customer base of people who watch what they eat. One smart option O'Naturals is pursuing is family meals to take home—similar to the Boston Market offer. **Rating =.**
3. Follow-up costs are extremely low at a restaurant as the people consume the product. **Rating +.**
4. The initial investment is high, but like Dr. Spock, it is justified by the significant size of the market. **Rating +.**
5. Funding to hold market share is probably out of reach of most start-up companies if the natural fast-food restaurant concept takes off. The company's position can usually be salvaged by selling out to a well-funded company. **Rating =.**
6. The investment required for new food entrees or the occasional remodeling is small, but promoting those changes is high. **Rating ?.**

Jawroski's Towing and Repair

Jawroski's Towing and Repair is a car repair/towing business in a fast-growing suburban area. One thing consumers soon learn is that there is always lots of maintenance that can be done on a car, and customers have to get the repair work done right. That is great for Jawroski's, as they have lots of possibilities for selling more services. Jawroski's has a high upfront investment with its high-tech diagnostic equipment, but once it's in, ongoing costs are modest.

Evaluation of Jawroski's potential for long life:

1. Auto repair shops typically have strong margins as long as their mechanics can complete work in a timely manner. **Rating +.**
2. Up-selling and cross-selling are naturals with mechanics who both want

to sell more services but also want customers to be aware of other problems in case the car suffers another quick breakdown. **Rating +.**

3. Jaworski's has to be careful to control its service quality and to control customers' expectations of the work performed in order to keep follow-up sales costs down. **Rating =.**

4. It's expensive to open up a car repair facility, but the cost is justified by the market size and the high profit margins of an auto repair facility. **Rating +.**

5. Funding to hold market share is usually not a problem for car repairs because consumers like to use a shop either near their home or where they work. There is a danger in losing fleet business, but Jawroski's has a big head start there as it already holds the business and has an excellent reputation. **Rating +.**

6. Auto repair shops have to invest to stay on the cutting edge, but the expense is usually minimal as all the major companies offer training classes and assist shops in getting equipment needed for the new cars they introduce. **Rating +.**

Don't Level the Field

eWork Markets (*www.eworkmarkets.com*) is a dotcom company that started from a $10,000 investment and has grown to serve over 17,000 clients with almost 100 employees. eWork Markets is an Internet matchmaker between consulting firms and end

G–Yes
E–Yes
L–Yes

users, which include Fortune 500 companies like Texaco and Hasbro. At first glance eWork doesn't seem to be much different than GiftCertificates.com. They have competition from Guru.com and other sites that connect consultants and companies and endless promotion seemed to be in their future.

But eWork realized that they would only succeed by staying on the cutting edge. They realized that firms had hundreds of consultants to choose from, but that they didn't always know the right firm to choose. eWorks stands out from competition by developing Internet-based tools and standards that helped companies select the right consultant for the right price for their firm. eWork succeeded with one of marketing's basic lessons: customers will locate you when you give them exactly what they want. Follow eWorks' approach for success. Don't try to out-promote the competition. Instead offer what prospects perceive to be a better package of services.

Chapter 8

Evaluating Your Concept

T HE REASON I'VE HEARD MOST FROM BUSINESS OWNERS FOR NOT doing a business plan is that things change too fast and a business plan is obsolete after just a few months. The business owners have a point. Plans do constantly change.

But the fact that things change is the very reason business owners need to do GEL factor analysis frequently. Whether they end up writing a plan is not as important as doing an analysis. I recommend you take a close look at your business concept, see its flaws, and then correct them as your business changes.

The big advantage of this approach is that flaws you find in your business concept can be corrected before they cost you any money. Those entrepreneurs writing a plan before doing a GEL factor analysis will probably eventually make the same changes that an entrepreneur doing a GEL factor analysis will make. But they'll make them only after they've learned by failing—a lesson that can be very expensive.

There are three steps involved in evaluating your concept:

1. Fill in your checklists.
2. Readjust your strategy.
3. Do the final tally.

Company Story—Not Always the First Choice

EC Outlook of Houston, Texas, has been chosen as one of *Inbound Logistics Magazine*'s Top 100 Logistics IT Providers, one of *Upside Magazine*'s Hot 100 companies, and one of *Computerworld*'s top 100 emerging companies to watch. EC Outlook provides e-business connectivity solutions—and today it's thriving.

G—Yes
E—Yes
L—Yes

EC Outlook is succeeding, but it's actually on its fourth business model concept. The company demonstrates the wisdom of the old adage, "If at first you don't succeed, try, try again." EC Outlook's technology is a solution for the problem of connecting companies, with widely varying internal software, through e-marketplaces and e-transactions. EC Outlook's solution is a translation package that converts files from varying formats into a format a communication partner can read.

EC Outlook's first idea was to sell its products to big companies. But that sale, and subsequent product support, was too complicated and expensive. Plan 2 was to provide conversion services and software to small companies. In this case, the amount of effort to sell small customers was too much for the revenue generated by the sales. The third choice was to sell a service to large companies that would convert incoming and outgoing data to and from small and mid-sized vendors that didn't have conversion capabilities. This was a big sale and relatively easy, as it eliminated a big problem for big companies: how to seamlessly connect to small and mid-sized vendors that have minimal technology capability. This model was successful for the company and it allowed it to move to a fourth business model, where it both provides conversion service and sells its conversion products.

EC Outlet's experience is typical of new start-ups: they frequently need to change their business model in order to succeed. The trick is to find the right model without spending a lot of money. Hopefully this chapter will help you make the changes you need without exhausting your resources.

Fill in Your Checklists

The first step in evaluating your concept is to fill in the checklists at the end of this chapter. As you're filling in these checklists, don't look at them as a matter of pass or fail. They're a starting point for fine-tuning your business concept, for adjusting the model to make it more effective. The next section of the chapter covers how to make adjustments when necessary. You may need to go through the checklist process several times, so you have permission to copy the checklists for those multiple uses. Remember: these checklists are used to help you create a winning strategy for your firm. Grading your model too high will only hurt you in the long run.

		Desired	Excellent	Average	Poor	Compensating Tactics Yes	No
GREAT CUSTOMERS							
Customer Characteristics	Number	High					
	Ease of Finding	Easy					
	Spending Patterns	Prolific					
Customer Value to Company	$ Value of Sale	High					
	Repeat Sales	Many					
	Ongoing Sales Support	Low					
EASY SALES							
Value to Customer	How Important	Important					
	Competitive Advantage	High					
	Price/Value Relationship	Low					
Customer Acquisition Cost	Entry Points	Many					
	Sales Support Required	Little					
	Promotional Activities	Low					
LONG LIFE							
Profit per Sale	Margins	High					
	Up-Selling and Cross-Selling	Much					
	Ongoing Product Costs	Low					
Investment Required	To Enter Business	Low					
	To Keep Market Share	Low					
	To Stay on the Cutting Edge	Low					

Figure 8-1. GEL Factor Checklist

The GEL factor checklist will give you an initial assessment of your concept. Objectively evaluate each point on the chart and check the box. For any of the key determinants in the business model evaluation in which your model rates a grade of "average" or "poor," consider compensating tactics.

		List Compensating Tactics	Effectiveness		
			1	2	3
GREAT CUSTOMERS					
Customer Characteristics	Number				
	Ease of Finding				
	Spending Patterns				
Customer Value to Company	$ Value of Sale				
	Repeat Sales				
	Ongoing Sales Support				
EASY SALES					
Value to Customer	How Important				
	Competitive Advantage				
	Price/Value Relationship				
Customer Acquisition Cost	Entry Points				
	Sales Support Required				
	Promotional Activities				
LONG LIFE					
Profit per Sale	Margins				
	Up-Selling and Cross-Selling				
	Ongoing Product Costs				
Investment Required	To Enter Business				
	To Keep Market Share				
	To Stay on the Cutting Edge				

Figure 8-2. Compensating Tactics

The Compensating Tactics checklist is a chart where you can list ways to compensate for the weak points of your business—any key element rated as "average" or "poor." A "poor" element needs one or more highly effective compensating tactics; an "average" element might get by with a mildly effective tactic or even without any compensating tactic.

I recommend that you do a little brainstorming exercise before filling out this chart. List at least four to five possible compensating tactics for each element where you rate your performance "average" or "poor." Next, let those tactics set for two to three days. Then, look at them again and try to list two to three other tactics you could use. Finally, wait another two days and chose the tactics you might consider using.

Success Tip

Most businesses I've worked with can't effectively implement more than three compensating tactics. You need to choose your tactics carefully, both in terms of what concerns you want to address and in terms of which tactics will have the most impact on your business. Consult with at least three or four customers to help you choose the right tactics. They will know which tactics will best help you overcome weaknesses in your business model.

		Winner	Average	Corrected	Concern
GREAT CUSTOMERS					
Customer Characteristics	Number				
	Ease of Finding				
	Spending Patterns				
Customer Value to Company	$ Value of Sales				
	Repeat Sales				
	Ongoing Sales Support				

Figure 8-3. Preliminary Evaluation Form (continued on next page)

		Winner	Average	Corrected	Concern
EASY SALES					
Value to Customer	How Important				
	Competitive Advantage				
	Ongoing Sales Support				
Customer Acquistion Cost	Entry Points				
	Sales Support Required				
	Promotional Activities				
LONG LIFE					
Profit per Sale	Margins				
	Up-Selling and Cross-Selling				
	Ongoing Product Costs				
Investment Required	To Enter Business				
	To Keep Market Share				
	To Stay on the Cutting Edge				

Figure 9-3. Preliminary Evaluation Form (continued)

The Preliminary Evaluation form provides an easy way for you to rate how you stand in regard to each element of the successful business model criteria. The "Concern" column is for weak elements of your business model where you can't implement a compensating tactic or where you can't be sure your compensating tactic will work. Of course you'd like all of your checkmarks to be in the "Winner" column, but I've never seen a concept have a winning rating in every category. But you definitely want your checkmarks to be clustered down the left side of the columns of this chart.

I believe that, in order to succeed, three of the six categories must be dominating winners and the other three must be average, at worst.

Must Have Winners		
Customers—Ease of Finding	_____Yes	All must be checked Yes or the model is flawed.
Value to Customer—Price/Value Relationship	_____Yes	
Profit per Sale—Margins	_____Yes	
Must Not Be a Concern		
Customers—Spending Patterns	_____No	All must be checked No or the model is flawed.
Customer Value to Company—Ongoing Sales Support	_____No	
Investment Required—To Keep Market Share	_____No	

Winners	Concerns
1._____	1._____
2._____	2._____
3._____	3._____
4._____	4._____
5._____	5._____
6._____	6._____
7._____	7._____
8._____	8._____
9._____	9._____

Winners need to outnumber concerns by three to one in order to proceed.

Figure 8-4. Final Evaluation Form

Readjust Your Strategy

I've found you can correct problems in your business model by evaluating four areas of your business strategy:

1. Change target customers.
2. Change the value to customers.

Pitfalls to Avoid

One of the biggest negatives I've ever heard from a venture capitalist about entrepreneurs is that they are "married to their idea"—which translates into "The entrepreneurs aren't going to listen to advice or make the changes necessary to make their business succeed." The chances of creating the ideal business model right from the start are slim. It's crucial for your success to evaluate and adjust your concept.

3. Change the sales/distribution strategy.
4. Change how the product/service is produced.

You may need changes in one area or you may decide to change all four. Try to make as few adjustments as possible, however, since a change in one area could create unanticipated concerns in other categories. For example, a change in your target customer could create a dramatic negative shift in your company's value proposition to customers.

Change Target Customers

You might need to look for new target customers for a wide number of reasons, including the following:

▶ You can't find enough of them.

▶ They don't spend freely.

▶ Your product isn't important enough to them.

▶ They are hard to acquire.

▶ They require too much sales support.

You simply cannot change a customer group's behavior, perceptions, or tendencies.

Change the Value/Importance to Customers

If you have the right customer group and the customers just aren't buying, you can do any or all of the following:

▶ Add features and/or services.

▶ Become a solution.

▶ Increase your competitive advantage.

The secret to figuring out how to change value and/or importance to customers is to understand what customers really want; the reasons why they buy. You need first-hand customer input; you cannot just pull together what you feel customers want. This is especially true for establishing a competitive advantage. You have an advantage only if you are offering features or solutions that count with the customers.

A simple way to get this information is to make up six to eight product or service offerings with different features and with varying progress toward a solution. You may need to do brochures for each product or service. Then ask customers these questions:

1. What was your first consideration when you evaluated each product?
2. What product would you rank first? Why?
3. What product would you rank last? Why?
4. What features/services would you like to see added?
5. What features/services would you like to see dropped?

Change Sales/Distribution Strategy

Sales and distribution strategy is probably the most important characteristic of any marketing program. It's also the category where you have far and away the most options. I've listed next some of the major problems you can correct with sales and distribution and some of the corrective measures you can take. Some of these problems can also be addressed with product feature changes.

1. **Customers are hard to locate.** Correction—sell through other companies or distributors that have already located these customers.
2. **Customers require high sales or ongoing product support.** Correction—sell through dealer networks or set a franchisee network to provide the support required.
3. **Customers don't perceive your product or service as being important.** Correction—sell through other manufacturers or set up a network where a total solution is provided.
4. **Customers make a slow decision.** Correction—sell through a network where your product is part of a more important choice.

Buzzword

"Distribution" is a term that people typically think of as being a sales channel, such as selling through distributors to retailers. But it really means any method you use to get your product to customers. For example, a business that holds seminars for inventors and then sells its products and services at those seminars has a distribution strategy—its seminars. Franchises, store location, and selling through other stores are all distribution strategies.

Change How the Product/Service Is Produced

In some cases, your model might have costs that are too high, resulting in margins that are just too low. For example, a software consulting service could have a complete staff, which is a high-cost option, or it might only have a few project managers on staff and then hire the independent contractors it needs for each job, which is a lower-cost option. Manufacturers in the United States frequently move production to lower-cost manufacturing outlets, either elsewhere in the country or overseas.

Do the Final Tally

Once you've made the final tally, you simply need to go back to the section, "Filling in Your Checklists." Recheck your score to be sure it is high enough. Once it is, wait at least one week and go over your business model again. With a fresh look you might be able to get a few more ideas on how your model could be further improved. Check your business model score at least every six months. You'll find out new things from the marketplace that might help you further refine your model.

Spending Rises Exponentially

I've found over the past 30 years that there is one business fact no one likes to discuss. That fact is that as your concept, solution, or tactic moves away from the ideal, your spending to make that tactic effective increases at what appears to be exponential rates. That is, if an ideal tactic takes $10 to implement, then even a modestly less ideal tactic takes anywhere from $50 to $100 to implement with equal effectiveness.

The tendency for many people is to gloss over deficiencies in their model and throw in compensating tactics. You should be cautious about compensating tactics, as it's difficult for any company to implement more than two or three of them effectively. A better solution is to keep reworking your business concept until you have one that better meets the successful business model criteria. My experience is that compensating tactics will, at the very best, be only half as effective as changing the model so that it meets the success criteria.

Section 1
Part Three

Business Concept Analysis:
Case Studies

Chapter 9

GEL Factor Analysis– Retail, Manufacturing, and Services

Retail Company: AutoFun–Almost but Not Quite Right

AUTOFUN WAS A SMALL CHAIN OF AUTO ACCESSORIES STORES THAT stayed in business about three years. The company offered fun items for cars, including neon light license plate holders, car stereos, seat covers, bike racks, funny gizmos for the top of the antennas, and car seat covers.

The company's founders felt that their competitive advantage was that no other store concentrated just on fun auto accessories. There are tons of auto parts stores, but they carry only a limited selection of accessories. Mass merchandisers such as Wal-Mart also carry auto accessories and there are several auto parts catalogs that carry accessories, but none that carry as many products as AutoFun. The store also had stiff competition from stereo retailers that offered a wide range of auto stereo equipment. AutoFun's founders felt that the market would like to have a store that people could visit often to see what was new in the market.

Pitfalls to Avoid

Impulse items, which would include many auto accessories, need to be seen to be purchased. That's why accessories sell well in an auto parts store. People are in the store to buy something else and see the accessory and buy it on impulse. They wouldn't have gone to a store just to buy the accessory. You can't really base a store on impulse items, which was part of the AutoFun model.

Strong Points

1. **Prolific spending.** AutoFun's target customers were people who love their cars. It's not uncommon for AutoFun's target customers to spend several thousand dollars pin-striping their cars right after they buy them. They buy things for their cars all the time and, theoretically, they would be willing to come back to the store repeatedly to purchase more products.
2. **High margins.** Retailers don't have to discount specialty products that can't be found anywhere else. High-end products with high margins are typically a winning formula. One of AutoFun's problems was that it just couldn't find enough high-end specialty products that weren't carried by other stores.

Weak Points

1. **Ease of finding the right customer.** AutoFun sold a broad range of products, including neon lights for license plates, car stereos, bike carriers, and fancy car seat covers. The problem was that different customers bought each of these products. For example, someone who wanted neon lights for his or her license plate probably wouldn't also be interested in buying a bike rack.
2. **Too few entry points.** Although there was a demand for AutoFun's products, since only a small percentage of people purchased its products, and purchased them infrequently, that meant that AutoFun could have only a limited number of stores in any metropolitan area. Its competitors—

Success Tip

When you do a GEL factor evaluation, you need to evaluate how you stack up against competition as you score each point. AutoFun's number of entry points was low in comparison with the number of entry points for auto parts and auto stereo stores, which were its major competitors. AutoFun's number of entry points might have been acceptable if its competitors also had a limited number of entry points.

		Desired	Excellent	Average	Poor	Compensating Tactics	
						Yes	No
GREAT CUSTOMERS							
Customer Characteristics	Number	High		✔			
	Ease of Finding	Easy			✔		
	Spending Patterns	Prolific	✔				
Customer Value to Company	$ Value of Sale	High		✔			
	Repeat Sales	Many			✔		
	Ongoing Sales Support	Low	✔				
EASY SALES							
Value to Customer	How Important	Important		✔			
	Competitive Advantage	High		✔			
	Price/Value Relationship	Low		✔			
Customer Acquisition Cost	Entry Points	Many			✔		
	Sales Support Required	Little		✔			
	Promotional Activities	Low			✔		
LONG LIFE							
Profit per Sale	Margins	High	✔				
	Up-Selling and Cross-Selling	Much			✔		
	Ongoing Product Costs	Low		✔			
Investment Required	To Enter Business	Low		✔			
	To Keep Market Share	Low		✔			
	To Stay on the Cutting Edge	Low		✔			

which included, on some products, mass merchandisers like Wal-Mart and, on other products, auto parts stores—had far more entry points.

3. **AutoFun couldn't discover any low-cost promotional activities.** Promotional costs are typically high whenever you don't have a tightly focused target customer group. You can't develop a reliable mailing list and you can't partner up with other companies that target the same customers. The result is that you have to market to a large group to find the small group of customers who may want to buy your product.

4. **Repeat sales happened infrequently.** AutoFun's products—whether a rear-mounted bike rack, a neon license plate light, or a car stereo—were purchases that people make only very occasionally. The result is that AutoFun could not count on a certain level of sales each month from repeat customers, but instead had to go out and get new customers all the time.

5. **Up-selling and cross-selling opportunities were limited.** Customers who buy neon license plates might also buy a car stereo, but probably not a bike rack or an office-in-the car product. Customers would likely find only one or two items in the store that they would consider purchasing.

Manufacturing Company: Coach—Meeting Customer Desires

Coach is a manufacturer of high-quality handbags that was losing market share in the late 90s to fashion designers that were starting to do handbags. Those companies benefited from cross-selling a handbag to customers buying some of their other fashion products.

Coach's response was to hire a top designer from Tommy Hilfiger and then create a "Lifestyle" brand by expanding its line to include a full range of designer products. Finally the company added new materials to its leather standard in the handbag line and reintroduced an old logo, C, to help demonstrate that its new line was cool. The results of the company's rejuvenation strategy were pretty cool, too. Sales increased from $500 to $700 million from 2002 to 2005, and continuing with the winning strategy, sales are expected to go over the $2 billion mark in 2007.

Pitfalls to Avoid

One of the dangers of being in a business like fashion, where a manufacturer is either "in fashion" or "out of fashion," is that the market is fickle and companies can't predict how customers will respond. Coach's decision to start offering more products is a response to this danger. Having a broader product line offers protection in case the market turns away from a company's main product.

Strong Points

1. **The target customers like to spend money.** There are a significant number of people who spend lots of money to keep looking good. If a company gets the "buzz" on its side, profits will be high.

		Desired	Excellent	Average	Poor	Compensating Tactics	
						Yes	No
GREAT CUSTOMERS							
Customer Characteristics	Number	High		✔			
	Ease of Finding	Easy		✔			
	Spending Patterns	Prolific	✔				
Customer Value to Company	$ Value of Sale	High	✔				
	Repeat Sales	Many	✔				
	Ongoing Sales Support	Low		✔			
EASY SALES							
Value to Customer	How Important	Important	✔				
	Competitive Advantage	High		✔			
	Price/Value Relationship	Low		✔			
Customer Acquisition Cost	Entry Points	Many		✔			
	Sales Support Required	Little		✔			
	Promotional Activities	Low		✔			
LONG LIFE							
Profit per Sale	Margins	High	✔				
	Up-Selling and Cross-Selling	Much		✔			
	Ongoing Product Costs	Low	✔				
Investment Required	To Enter Business	Low			✔	✔	
	To Keep Market Share	Low		✔			
	To Stay on the Cutting Edge	Low			✔		✔

2. **The purchase is important.** Looking good matters a lot to the target customer group. That means that people will look at different products as they become available and that they are willing to switch brands for a new, better look. Also, when a purchase is important, people also look at what other people are doing, which means a current customer could encourage many other people to check out a new fashion. The importance of the purchase is also why there are so many fashion magazines

that cover the new styles. Moving into a more important purchase category was a major improvement over the company's old model, where it sold only leather handbags.

3. **The dollar value of the sale is high.** High fashion certainly equals high dollars. Expanding the product line also gives the company a better chance to sell more products. Having a higher dollar value also helps Coach succeed with fewer retailers. The company can work closer with its key retailers and develop better programs to promote sales.

4. **Strong potential for repeat sales.** Customers might buy a handbag and then come back to get a dress or fashion accessory to match the handbag. Plus they might remember a designer they like when they get ready to buy a new product. This again is an improvement over the old model. The target customers might have a selection of handbags, but it won't be nearly as large as their collection of clothes.

5. **High fashion typically equals high margins.** Part of the appeal of high fashion is that it is expensive and that most people can't or won't buy it—but high profits can be made from people who do buy.

Success Tip

High margins provide a second benefit; they allow Coach to give its retailers lots of support to help sell its products. Manufacturers with high margins can offer retailers upscale displays, sales catalogs, special mailing pieces, and other promotional materials to help sell their products. Companies do best when they invest part of their high margins back into marketing to build the brand and help their retailers.

Weak Points

1. **Establishing a brand name in fashion is expensive and difficult.** The main reason for this is that there are so many fashion retailers. One advantageous factor for Coach was that it had already established a brand name in fashion handbags. A compensating tactic for Coach was that it hired a "hot" designer away from Tommy Hilfiger, one of the market's leading names, to lead its new products team.

2. **Staying on the leading edge is expensive and challenging.** There's no way around the fact that staying on top is risky when you sell to a market that is based solely on desires and image and not on any true functional product needs. The whims of the market swing quickly and a company's market share can drop in a big hurry. The customers can choose from many businesses and competition is fierce.

Service Company: Everdream—Meeting a Big Need

Everdream provides a type of service called *subscription computing*. Everdream provides software, computers, printers, networking, and everything else a company might need for computing for $200 to $350 per month per user. Its target market is small to mid-sized businesses that can't afford a big upfront fee for computer purchases or simply don't want to waste time configuring and setting up new programs, computers, or networks. Everdream also offers 24/7 technical support, automated online backup, virus protection, maintenance and repair, and unlimited DSL web access with e-mail and service guarantees. Everdream allows companies to upgrade their equipment anytime after the first 12 months for a fee. Everdream boasts that in many cases companies that have five or six users would pay more to consultants to set up their computers than they pay to actually have the equipment installed, and up and running with Everdream. The company offers its services through its own web site and sales force but primarily relies on resellers, who are established computer solutions providers to businesses that have an existing customer base and sales force.

Buzzwords

Subscription providers provide access to high technology and support for a monthly fee, including both hardware and software. *Application service providers* (ASPs) provide only software for a monthly fee. Customers don't have to worry about equipment or software updates or how to integrate new technology into their existing business because the provider takes care of this for them. Both types of services promote trouble-free computing as their main benefit.

Strong Points

1. **A high number of potential customers.** Everdream's target customers are small to mid-sized companies with a low level of computer expertise. This group includes probably over half of small to mid-sized companies. An Everdream salesperson could probably drive down any industrial street and find several companies interested in its services.
2. **Current technology is critical for many small businesses.** In fact, technology is becoming more and more important, especially with the emergence of online marketplaces for businesses and the move by many large companies to web-enable their technology.

		Desired	Excellent	Average	Poor	Compensating Tactics	
						Yes	No
GREAT CUSTOMERS							
Customer Characteristics	Number	High	✔				
	Ease of Finding	Easy		✔			
	Spending Patterns	Prolific		✔			
Customer Value to Company	$ Value of Sale	High		✔			
	Repeat Sales	Many	✔				
	Ongoing Sales Support	Low			✔	✔	
EASY SALES							
Value to Customer	How Important	Important	✔				
	Competitive Advantage	High	✔				
	Price/Value Relationship	Low		✔			
Customer Acquisition Cost	Entry Points	Many		✔			
	Sales Support Required	Little		✔			
	Promotional Activities	Low		✔			
LONG LIFE							
Profit per Sale	Margins	High		✔			
	Up-Selling and Cross-Selling	Much	✔				
	Ongoing Product Costs	Low			✔	✔	
Investment Required	To Enter Business	Low			✔		
	To Keep Market Share	Low	✔				
	To Stay on the Cutting Edge	Low		✔			

3. The company has a big advantage for its customers over the traditional route businesses take to acquire technology—buying the equipment on their own. Most small businesses don't want or can't deal with all the complexities of today's interconnected world. Setting up so a salesperson can access in-house data while on the World Wide Web is just one of the smaller challenges. Providing a turnkey solution is an enormous advantage and Everdream has only a few competitors in the subscription market.

4. **High percentage of repeat sales because of the monthly fee.** One of the advantages of a monthly fee is that people keep buying without having to make a new purchase decision. Upgrades are completed for a low cost and increase in the monthly fee, a much easier decision to make for a business than going out and buying a new set of equipment and software and then having to figure out how to get it working.

5. **There are many opportunities for cross-selling and up-selling.** Selling new software and hardware is relatively easy: first, because Everdream's monthly fee makes the buying decision relatively pain-free and, second, because the company is constantly in contact with its customers, providing technical service.

6. **The company's distribution strategy makes it easy to keep market share.** Everdream sells through solutions-based resellers, which like selling the product because it gives them another tool to use when selling small businesses. There are many of these firms in the market, they have established good reputations, and they have a customer base already in place.

Pitfalls to Avoid

Many new companies with a strong business model like Everdream's seem to think people will just buy because their offer is so good. That's simply not true. Sales and distribution are always a key element in any company's success and you have to commit resources to sell your product. Everdream's alliances with solutions providers as its reseller network are another strong point in the GEL factor analysis.

Weak Points

1. **High ongoing sales support.** Everdream's customers are facing a rapidly changing technology world and they will have lots of questions for Everdream about what to do next. Everdream accepted this cost and simply built the costs of sales support into its monthly fee. The upside of the sales support is that it allows Everdream many opportunities for up-selling and cross-selling.

2. **High ongoing product costs.** One reason that Everdream's service is interesting to its customers is that the cost of upgrading technology is high. The cost is also high for Everdream. Everdream can mitigate this risk by leasing equipment, and it is able to cover the lease costs in its monthly fee. The costs are a concern, though, if business turns down, and those costs could put the company in jeopardy if Everdream is caught holding excess inventory.

3. **High cost of entering the business.** This is good news and bad news. The bad news is that high costs make it challenging for Everdream to build up a nationwide network of resellers. The good news is that if Everdream, as one of the earliest companies in the market, can gain strong initial market share, the high cost of entering will make it difficult for competitors to enter the market.

Small Business: American Wildlife Art Galleries–Drawing Customers

The popularity of wildlife art has been increasing over the last 10 years, with works by major artists regularly selling for anywhere from $20,000 to $50,000. The American Wildlife Art Galleries originally sold a variety of artists, but when a new owner took over, he focused on the wildlife art of Les C. Kouba, one of the founders of the wildlife art genre, who died in 1998. To bring the prices down to a level that was more affordable to most people, the store starting reproducing the paintings using a process that prints the pictures onto canvas. The owner limits the reproductions to 750 to 1,000 of each painting. The reproductions sell for about $600 each. The owner also produces prints of the paintings that range in price from $30 for a small-sized print to more than $100 for a full-sized print. In addition, the store sells T-shirts, playing cards, plaques, and other products based on Kouba's work. Since Kouba produced thousands of paintings, the store has an unlimited number of potential pictures to work with. The gallery is the ninth floor of an office building in downtown Minneapolis, a location somewhat out of the way for some, and operates with two employees. The business is a success because the gallery appeals to people who love wildlife art but aren't in a position to pay the high prices of original work.

Success Fact

People devoted to a hobby, avocation, or interest are always an ideal customer group. They will look for a business in odd places and visit frequently a business devoted to their interest. Best of all, they are willing to spend money on their interest. The only question for a small business is whether or not there are enough devoted people in the area to support it.

		Desired	Excellent	Average	Poor	Compensating Tactics	
						Yes	No
GREAT CUSTOMERS							
Customer Characteristics	Number	High		✔			
	Ease of Finding	Easy	✔				
	Spending Patterns	Prolific	✔				
Customer Value to Company	$ Value of Sale	High	✔				
	Repeat Sales	Many	✔				
	Ongoing Sales Support	Low	✔				
EASY SALES							
Value to Customer	How Important	Important	✔				
	Competitive Advantage	High	✔				
	Price/Value Relationship	Low		✔			
Customer Acquisition Cost	Entry Points	Many			✔	✔	
	Sales Support Required	Little		✔			
	Promotional Activities	Low		✔			
LONG LIFE							
Profit per Sale	Margins	High	✔				
	Up-Selling and Cross-Selling	Much	✔				
	Ongoing Product Costs	Low		✔			
Investment Required	To Enter Business	Low			✔	✔	
	To Keep Market Share	Low		✔			
	To Stay on the Cutting Edge	Low	✔				

Strong Points

1. **Easy to find customers.** Wildlife art enthusiasts can be found through hunting and wildlife art magazines and through art shows and exhibits that concentrate on wildlife art. The store didn't need to run an expensive ad or promotional campaign to the general public.
2. **Customers enjoy buying wildlife art.** People who enjoy wildlife art are willing to buy it, especially when it is at an affordable price.

3. **Prices of prints and reproductions are a more affordable option.** Although there are some prints and reproductions of wildlife art available, most galleries concentrate on selling the more expensive originals or prints by lesser-known artists. The gallery has a big advantage in its Minneapolis location, since Les Kouba was a Minnesota artist.

Pitfalls to Avoid

Kouba was a Minnesota artist who also happened to have a nationwide reputation. Often businesses try to prosper from a local angle, such as a shop of Colorado merchandise. Those stores do well with tourists, provided that tourists can find them, but often local people won't shop there. A local connection alone is not enough; the merchandise still has to succeed on its own merits.

4. **Dollar value for each sale is significant.** The lowest-priced art in the store is small prints for $30 to $50. These still amount to a significant sale. Some people purchase accessories only, but those sales still easily exceed $10.
5. **Wildlife art devotees buy art on a regular basis.** One of the positive points of serving a market where people indulge their hobbies or avocations is that people keep on buying and expanding their collections. This repeat business also generate word-of-mouth advertising, since each wildlife art enthusiast likely knows four or five others.
6. **Very little ongoing sales support is required.** One of the nice things about selling art is that it doesn't require ongoing training, interfacing, or support. Once it is sold, people hang it on a wall and pretty much nothing can go wrong.
7. **Margins are relatively high.** High-quality artwork typically is sold at a margin of at least 50 percent, sometimes much higher. The question about quality artwork is not how much money is made per sale, but rather how many sales can be made.
8. **There are many up-selling and cross-selling opportunities.** One of the great features of this business concept is that wildlife art enthusiasts tend to prefer the art of a select number of people. So, if they buy one item, there's a chance they will buy another.
9. **The store will have a relatively easy time staying on the cutting edge.** Kouba created thousands of works of art and he passed away in 1998; people tend to appreciate an artist more the longer he or she is in the public eye. The store just needs to keep coming up with prints from different pictures, something it should be able to do without much trouble.

Weak Points

1. **There are only three entry points—a store, an Internet site, and eBay sales.** The store is in an unusual retail location that people need to look for in order to find. The mitigating factor is that the owner has a distinctive strategy and product line that has very strong appeal for his target customer group.

Success Tip

Retailers really have two entry points to worry about: first, how easy it is to find the store and, second, how many price points the store has. A wide variety of price points offers opportunities for every visitor to at least buy something. The store meets this second criterion with T-shirts, mugs, and other lower-cost accessories that people can buy that reflect their interest in wildlife art.

---

2. **Acquiring original paintings can be difficult and expensive.** The store was able to overcome this problem because the original shop owner was the nephew of Les Kouba. He was able to acquire a collection of original paintings from family and friends to launch the shop.

Small Business: Creative Indoor Billboards—Signs of Success

This firm from Sacramento, California, sells those billboards you find in restrooms in restaurants, sports bars, nightclubs, sports arenas, and other popular venues. The company is somewhat successful, with billboards in 150 locations. The ads cost anywhere from $100 to $2,000 per month, depending on the number of locations an advertiser takes, with the average customer paying about $400 per month. Monthly sales total about $50,000. Creative Indoor Billboards is offering access to a target customer group, young adults usually less than 35 who frequent nightclubs and bars. This target customer group is somewhat hard to promote to using traditional means because they don't have trade shows, magazines, or other venues that they attend, read, or go to regularly and, as a result, there are few really attractive advertising alternatives. They also don't qualify as steady TV viewers, either of cable shows or local programs.

Creative Indoor Billboards' target customers are not the young adults, but rather the advertisers that are trying to reach those young adults. The company finds its customers either because they see an ad in the restroom and call for more information or by searching ads in magazines, ads at movie theaters, direct-mail pieces, and other advertising from companies trying to reach the young adult market.

		Desired	Excellent	Average	Poor	Compensating Tactics Yes	No
GREAT CUSTOMERS							
Customer Characteristics	Number	High		✔			
	Ease of Finding	Easy	✔				
	Spending Patterns	Prolific		✔			
Customer Value to Company	$ Value of Sale	High		✔			
	Repeat Sales	Many		✔			
	Ongoing Sales Support	Low			✔		
EASY SALES							
Value to Customer	How Important	Important	✔				
	Competitive Advantage	High		✔			
	Price/Value Relationship	Low		✔			
Customer Acquisition Cost	Entry Points	Many		✔			
	Sales Support Required	Little			✔		
	Promotional Activities	Low		✔			
LONG LIFE							
Profit per Sale	Margins	High		✔			
	Up-Selling and Cross-Selling	Much		✔			
	Ongoing Product Costs	Low		✔			
Investment Required	To Enter Business	Low		✔			
	To Keep Market Share	Low		✔			
	To Stay on the Cutting Edge	Low		✔			

> ## Buzzword
>
> *High average sale* relates the sales value to the amount of sales effort required. It's a subjective term. For a retailer, $40 to $50 is a threshold for a high average sale. A company that sends local salespeople into the field might feel $10,000 is a high average sale. When salespeople travel, a starting figure for a high average sale is $20,000. If multiple sales calls are required, the high average sales number climbs even higher.

Strong Points

1. **Customers should be easy to find.** Creative Indoor Billboards' customers are people who try to reach young adults. They can find those people by simply observing where companies trying to reach those target customers advertise or promote their business.

2. **Companies need new, innovative ways to find customers.** The advertisers' target customers, young adults, can be difficult to reach simply because they are active and may not read magazines or newspapers or even watch the same shows repeatedly. That results in the advertisers always being interested in new cost-effective ways of reaching customers. They are willing to try new techniques because it's difficult for them to reach their customers.

Weak Points

1. **Lots of sales effort is required to make sales.** People are overwhelmed by the amount of advertising and information overload that they receive. As a result, ads are no longer as effective. This is exactly why Creative Indoor Billboards' customers are looking for new ways to reach customers. It is also the reason that it requires a lot of sales effort to sell each ad.

2. **Lots of ongoing sales effort is required to keep customers buying.** One of the problems marketers have with advertising is that it might take six months to see any results; and then, even when results are obtained, they are difficult to measure. For example, four people who join a health club might mention that they saw an ad in a restaurant, but the ad might have influenced many other new members. Advertising salespeople have to keep in constant touch with their customers or they will find that customers will get discouraged and drop their ad.

Small Business: Terri's Consign and Design Furnishings—Value and Prices

The first store in this chain opened in Arizona in 1979 with a $2,000 investment and now there are 16 stores throughout the country. Thrift stores and consignment shops are common, but Terri's does it with a twist. It offers only high- to very high-end furniture. It also supplements its merchandise with new overstock from major furniture manufacturers and stores that go out of business. The focus of the stores is offering distinctive merchandise that will make a home décor sizzle. Consignment merchandise is easy to obtain if the stores are located in upscale neighborhoods. The furniture typically has little wear and it offers a welcome addition to the homes of many middle-income families who want to have furnishings that can make a fashion statement.

Success Tip

One of the reasons for Terri's success is she realizes her business depends on having merchandise that brings people back. So her stores are in upscale neighborhoods where it's easier to get the consignment goods she is looking for. It would have been a mistake to locate the store where the customers live, as it would be harder to find consignment goods. Consider all aspects of your business before making a decision on where to locate.

Strong Points

1. **Customers are easy to find.** People with high, but not super-high, incomes who want upscale home furnishings can be found by buying a list of home décor magazines targeted at interior designers, getting the names of people who visit the upscale furniture marts that cater to interior designers, or using customer lists at upscale restaurants or gift shops. One of the other big advantages Terri's had was a lot of word-of-mouth advertising. People desiring a designer look often desire it because they like to entertain. Their friends probably also like to entertain and, as a result, just might be stopping at Terri's in the future.

2. **The purchase of upscale furniture is important.** Terri's targets customers who want an upscale room décor on a modest budget. Having that designer look and feel to a room is an important lifestyle choice for Terri's customers and they are willing to go far out of their way to get the merchandise they want.

		Desired	Excellent	Average	Poor	Compensating Tactics Yes	No
GREAT CUSTOMERS							
Customer Characteristics	Number	High		✔			
	Ease of Finding	Easy	✔				
	Spending Patterns	Prolific		✔			
Customer Value to Company	$ Value of Sale	High		✔			
	Repeat Sales	Many		✔			
	Ongoing Sales Support	Low		✔			
EASY SALES							
Value to Customer	How Important	Important	✔				
	Competitive Advantage	High	✔				
	Price/Value Relationship	Low	✔				
Customer Acquisition Cost	Entry Points	Many		✔			
	Sales Support Required	Little		✔			
	Promotional Activities	Low		✔			
LONG LIFE							
Profit per Sale	Margins	High			✔	✔	
	Up-Selling and Cross-Selling	Much	✔				
	Ongoing Product Costs	Low			✔		
Investment Required	To Enter Business	Low		✔			
	To Keep Market Share	Low		✔			
	To Stay on the Cutting Edge	Low		✔			

3. **The store has a competitive price advantage over high-end stores and a competitive product advantage over stores with similar prices.** Terri's is in an enviable position of having an advantage over both upscale stores, due to price, and mid-priced stores, due to the quality and look of the furniture she carries.

4. **The price/value relationship is excellent.** Terri's target customers are people who want designer furniture but can't afford it. Her product has the

best value for the money of any store selling high-end furniture and it's the only way for some customers to acquire the furniture they really want.

5. **There are many opportunities for up-selling or cross-selling.** One of the great things about selling furniture is that people also need lots of accessories to make the room look complete. Those accessories are a great tool for increasing the dollar value of every customer sale.

Pitfalls to Avoid

Accessories sell well because they complement the original purchase. Often businesses make the mistake of taking accessories lightly and not always making sure the merchandise complements the main product line. That mistake not only loses sales the company could have made, but also probably sticks the business with unwanted inventory. Choose your accessories just as carefully as you choose your principal products.

Weak Points

1. **Margins are lower than for most retail stores.** Consignment shops might get a 20 or 25 percent commission, versus a margin of 50 percent or higher at most furniture stores. Of course, Terri's doesn't have to buy the furniture, which keeps her costs down. But Terri still has all the other expenses associated with selling a product, such as marketing, sales, and administrative costs like bookkeeping, legal fees, and license costs.

2. **The cost of acquiring merchandise can be high.** Terri's depends on consistently having new consignment furniture in stock. The store needs an active campaign to acquire that stock. Terri's will also have to spend marketing dollars to promote her store to the people who will eventually buy her merchandise.

Internet Business: Webvan Group—Online Grocer

Webvan of San Francisco, launched in 1999, was one of the originators of the online grocery concept, where people order groceries online and have them delivered to their homes. The company was able to sign up 750,000 customers in its target markets of San Francisco, Los Angeles, Orange County (CA), San Diego, Seattle, Chicago, and Portland. The company burned through $830 million and closed in the summer of 2001 without ever turning a profit. Webvan failed despite having a 46 percent share and

Why Margins Count

A business with a 40 percent margin pays $60 to acquire or make goods that it sells for $100. The margin number is before sales and marketing, administration, and other costs are taken out to determine an actual profit percentage for a business. If a company has a 40 percent margin, it generates $40 in profit for a $100 sale. At a 30 percent margin, the company has to sell $133 to generate that same $40 in profit. That's a 33 percent increase in sales. What makes the situation even more unfavorable for the low-margin business is that sales and marketing costs typically run as a percentage of sales. I've listed below what happens to the margins after sales and marketing costs are taken out. Company A has a 40 percent margin and Company B has a 30 percent margin.

	Company A	Company B
Sales	$100	$133
Margin	40	40
Sales and Marketing Costs (15% of sales)	15	20
Margin after Sales and Marketing	25	20

The low-margin company not only has to sell more products but it typically still makes less money. Don't buy into the theory that you can accept making less money per product and then make up for the lower margin by selling more products. A company with a strong business concept always has a strong margin position. The only viable long-term tactic for having lower prices is to have lower costs.

sales of $77 million in the first quarter of 2001. It failed because it lost $218 million in that same quarter.

Webvan's problem was that it targeted too many customers. Rather than concentrating on customers who were willing to pay the $10 to $15 (if not more) it cost to deliver groceries, the company wanted a bigger market, people who wanted groceries delivered without paying a delivery charge. This was dangerous because it had to match prices with grocery stores, which are traditionally a very low-margin business. There was no way that Webvan could afford to deliver products for free and still charge the same price as grocery stores and make money. Webvan needed to charge for the convenience of delivery. Unfortunately, Webvan placed a premium on the number of customers it acquired, a strategy that dictated that Webvan not charge. The resulting business collapse was inevitable, because its business concept was flawed. The only way for Webvan to succeed was to be able to sell other, higher-margin products to the same customers. Even that strategy might not have overcome the drawback of losing $10 to $15 per customer every time the company delivered groceries.

Pitfalls to Avoid

One of the comments I commonly hear from failed businesses is that they ran out of money. And that certainly can be a problem. But sometimes before struggling businesses go out to raise more money, they should first make sure they have a business concept that has a chance to produce profits. You'll never have enough money to successfully launch a bad business idea.

Strong Points

1. **Everybody buys groceries—and many of those people dislike grocery shopping.** Working people come home tired and don't particularly care to go shopping in a crowded grocery store. But they need to eat. The number of potential customers is very high, possibly 25 percent of the total U.S. population, which is why Webvan was able to sign up 750,000 customers.
2. **People who would rather not grocery shop are easy to locate.** Webvan was able to promote its services to two-income professional families and easily locate plenty of prospective customers.
3. **The concept of having groceries delivered at no charge or for only a small charge is a major advantage over traditional grocery stores.** People who are busy aren't interested in taking one to two hours out of their day to go grocery shopping. Adding two hours of free time a week is a big advantage to a busy professional.
4. **Repeat sales are high, as people typically buy groceries at least once a week.** People have to keep eating and they have to keep shopping. Once customers discover they enjoy the convenience of online shopping, they are likely to keep using Webvan's service.

Weak Points

1. **The margins on groceries are just too small to support a business without a large delivery fee.** Webvan charged a fee for delivery, but it was way below its cost. Webvan had to take an order, send a person out to

		Desired	Excellent	Average	Poor	Compensating Tactics Yes	No
GREAT CUSTOMERS							
Customer Characteristics	Number	High	✔				
	Ease of Finding	Easy	✔				
	Spending Patterns	Prolific		✔			
Customer Value to Company	$ Value of Sale	High		✔			
	Repeat Sales	Many	✔				
	Ongoing Sales Support	Low		✔			
EASY SALES							
Value to Customer	How Important	Important		✔			
	Competitive Advantage	High	✔				
	Price/Value Relationship	Low	✔				
Customer Acquisition Cost	Entry Points	Many		✔			
	Sales Support Required	Little		✔			
	Promotional Activities	Low		✔			
LONG LIFE							
Profit per Sale	Margins	High			✔		
	Up-Selling and Cross-Selling	Much		✔			
	Ongoing Product Costs	Low		✔	✔		
Investment Required	To Enter Business	Low			✔		
	To Keep Market Share	Low			✔		
	To Stay on the Cutting Edge	Low		✔			

Success Tip

Many entrepreneurs dismiss cost-based pricing in favor of market-based pricing. But cost-based pricing has its place. When Webvan started, the owners should have determined what fee they needed to collect for each delivery and then determined what customer group would have been willing to pay that price. That is the customer group, then, that Webvan should have targeted.

fill the order, deliver the order, and finally collect the money. Owners of a grocery store just put the merchandise on the shelves.

2. **The costs to enter the business were high.** As a rule, Internet companies are less expensive to start than brick-and-mortar businesses. But for Webvan, just the opposite was true. The company needed a warehouse in each market, an order entry system capable of handling a large number of orders, people to fill the orders, delivery drivers, and delivery vans. That all amounts to a huge cost to enter the market.

3. **Costs to keep market share are high.** One of the difficult aspects of an Internet business is that its success heavily depends on customer awareness of the site. That means that a successful business can be copied by a larger, well-funded company that will take business away from the company with the business idea. To keep market share, an Internet company has to be prepared to keep spending money on customer awareness.

Section 2
Part One

The Business Plan:
Understanding
the Parts

Chapter 10

Executing a Successful Business Concept

O nce you have used the GEL factor analysis to fine-tune your business model concept, in most cases you'll want to put it into a plan. A plan is the most effective way to put your business concept into practice. Unfortunately most of the established businesses I work with don't write a new business plan unless they need to raise money. If you ask most business owners for a business plan, they will often tell you that there might be one around from four or five years ago. Or they might tell you they have a plan they did for a bank, but that their companies are not actually following the plan. I've separated this book into two sections to combat that attitude. At a minimum, business owners need to consider ways to upgrade their business model every year using GEL factors. While a good model is absolutely necessary to a good business, a good business plan greatly helps you to successfully execute that model. Following a business model without a plan is much like trying to build a house without blueprints: you may be able to do it, but not nearly as successfully.

Six Reasons

Just because owners don't always do a plan doesn't mean there aren't important reasons for doing so. Here are just a few of the reasons why:

1. **To get financing.** No matter how successful a business is, it won't be able to raise money without a business plan with a full set of financial projections for investors, banks, and even potential business partners.

2. **To communicate your company's strategy.** Employees are much more productive when they have a clear understanding of a business's objective and strategy. You should not minimize this need for communication. In some of the companies I've consulted with I found considerable disagreement among employees about issues as fundamental as what customers the company was targeting.

3. **As a development tool.** A business plan works out the details of how a business concept will be implemented, including the anticipation of problems that might emerge.

4. **As a resource planner.** New personnel, finances, manufacturing capacity, and inventory are just a few of a company's resources that a thoughtfully prepared business plan can specify.

5. **As a standard for evaluation.** How do investors and management decide if the company has had a good year? The business plan lays out what a company hopes to accomplish and provides a baseline for determining how well management or the company's owner has done to meet those goals.

6. **To set a budget.** Monthly revenue and expense budgets are two essential tools for companies to track performance and use for planning during the year. The budget and projections are keys that investors follow closely to judge performance.

Plans Can Vary

Businesses use a plan as a working document that gets modified, if not in the plan itself, at least in its implementation, based on changing situations and circumstances in the market or in a company's operations.

Realistically, businesses use a plan as a working document that gets modified, if not in the plan itself, at least in its implementation, based on changing situations and circumstances in the market or in a company's operations. Therefore a business plan needs to communicate a philosophy, why you are in business, commonly called a "mission statement," what factors point to success, and how you plan on approaching the market to take advantage of the opportunity before you. The four key elements of any business plan are: customers with a pronounced need or desire; a product or service to meet that need or desire; a cost-effective strategy for bringing that product or service to customers; and finally people in management with the expertise to make it all work.

You don't have to follow a business plan format exactly, and you have the freedom to tell your story any way you want. The only exception to this rule is the financial section and capitalization structure, which explains who owns how much of the company and how the ownership percentages will change when the company acquires new investors. These sections are particularly important if you are raising money either from investors or banks. I've deliberately chosen a sample plan in Chapter 18 that doesn't closely follow my suggested format, so readers can see the flexibility they have in creating a business plan. The financials listed in that plan are more comprehensive than usual because the plan is written to receive a bank loan. The plan I've included throughout Chapters 11 through 17 is written to receive money from angel investors, and fewer financials are required.

A business plan, no matter what its purpose, has to have a simple underlying story that investors, employees, and bankers can understand. The story needs to explain why the business makes sense and should succeed. A great plan will have two to three sentences that explain the entire essence of the business. A sample is: "The AutoV Editor targets the major manufacturers of digital camcorders, cameras, and camera phones. The AutoV Editor's easy-to-use video editing gives these potential customers a major market advantage as their products could offer instant editing to the 85 percent of the public who have never edited their videos or pictures, primarily because they find the editing process intimidating." I recommend you write these two to three tell-all sentences before starting the plan.

Company Goals

One last point a business plan must make clear is an overriding goal for the company. The goal is important for investors, bankers, and employees. One goal entrepreneurs have in raising money is to show rapid market growth with an exit plan so investors can get their money out. You should also translate that goal into measurable goals for the employees. For example, you want the company to dominate a market, gain 10 percent market share, become the preferred supplier to five customers, or establish a partnership network that provides nationwide sales coverage.

Many businesses doing plans are borrowing money with an SBA or bank loan, or writing a plan to help operate the company, and they often have more limited goals than a company looking to go public in a few years.

One goal entrepreneurs have in raising money is to show rapid market growth with an exit plan so investors can get their money out.

125

Pitfalls to Avoid

I talk to business owners all the time who don't write a plan because they "have it all in their head." This is a big mistake. The advantage of a plan is that it forces you to look at opportunities, market changes, and potential strategies before those factors impact your business. Business owners who have the plan in their head typically don't react until sales dramatically fall off, at which time it might be too late to turn the situation around.

Those owners just want to develop a business that will grow to produce a steady income. For example, an engineer at a company that does machining work might see that the market needs a better product to collect the mist that develops from cutting oil. The engineer's goal might just be to develop a business with the potential of $1 million in annual sales. The short-term goals might be to complete product development and sign on 15 distributors to carry the product.

Other entrepreneurs start a service or retail business based on changes to the market, the success of similar businesses, or their past job experience. These individuals typically have a goal of first positioning their business so they have advantages over competitors, either in location, product offerings, pricing, or service, and then establishing a customer base capable of generating a certain income level per year.

Comprehensive but Concise

You never want to treat a business plan lightly, especially if you're trying to raise money. The way your plan is written says something about you and the company's management style. Your plan needs to be thorough and comprehensive but at the same time it has to show that you can discern and focus on key elements of your business.

Success tips

Pie charts and graphs are tools often used in plans to show facts like market share. Charts can be quite useful when lots of information needs to be communicated concisely. For example, you can show the differences between your product or service and those of your competitors with a chart that shows what features each product has. The buying patterns of targeted customer groups can also be easily shown in a chart.

I've found that people who really understand their business can come to the heart of the matter quickly. They don't ramble on, and they focus on the issues that the company has to address to succeed. One of the biggest mistakes entrepreneurs make, especially if they are trying to land investors, is to list too many supporting facts to make a point. I've seen plans with as many as 9 or 10 facts to support one point. Avoid redundancy and too many facts at all costs. Remember instead the two- or three-sentence description of your business I recommended writing earlier in the chapter. Communicate precisely and clearly.

Chapter 11

The Executive Summary

The executive summary of your business plan offers a capsule view of your plan, hopefully in no more than 1,000 words. The executive summary is the most important part of the plan, for two reasons. First, it's the only part of the plan many investors will read in order to decide if they want to talk with you. Second, most people won't continue to read the plan if the executive summary doesn't catch their attention. You should have almost every sentence in the summary make a new point and you need to avoid long explanations for any one item.

What to Communicate

1. **The essence of the venture.** Business owners tend to know their business too well and assume that other people will understand it right away. This is a major mistake if you have a business that is new or out of the ordinary. My experience is that 50 percent of the time people reading a business plan summary of a new business don't understand the business concept. I recommend that you give people three sentences, of not more than 40 words, that describe your business. Ask people to read those words and explain what your business is. If they can't do that, you need to work harder on describing your business.

2. **Your unique or special opportunity.** You obviously decided to go into the particular business because something about it appealed to you. That appeal is what you want to express. Perhaps your location is special, you have access to special merchandise or technology, you have an alliance with a key person or company, or you are in a unique position to solve your customers' problems or help them meet their desires.

Success Tip

Even though the executive summary is the first part of the plan, I've found it works best to write the summary last. Most writers are a little fuzzy about exactly how the plan will come out when they start writing the plan. Their thinking crystallizes as they write, which will make it much easier to write the summary and ensure that the summary matches the points of the plan.

---

3. **Management's goals.** No matter who your audience is—investors, bankers, or employees—they all are concerned about just what your goals are. I've found that everyone reading the plan wants to see an ambitious goal, not necessarily in terms of sales, but certainly in terms of market share. One company I worked with had a goal of achieving 1 percent market share after two years. That goal doesn't inspire anyone. Your market share goal could be for just one state or just one market, but be sure the goal represents a significant achievement. I've found that everyone reading a plan looks for some passion, some ambition, and some dedication in the business owner or management team. You'll never convince someone you have that if your goal is not at least moderately ambitious.

Format

Your summary does not need to follow this exact format, but you should be sure it covers these points.

1. **Description.** Start the section with the name of the company, what type of company it is (i.e., sole proprietorship, Subchapter S, partnership, or other), and where the company is located. People will often also state how old the business is.
2. **Concept.** In 40 words or less, state your business concept. Most plans consolidate the description and the concept into an Introduction section. State how you will make revenue, if there's any doubt possible. For

example, dotcom companies might make revenue from sales, ads, links, or affiliate agreements.

Buzzword

"Space" is a recent term used by venture capitalists and investors. It's what used to be called a "market niche." Examples of *space* might be top-of-the-line mountain bikes for high-end consumers, e-commerce solutions for medical companies, or software solutions for music store inventory management. To catch the full definition of a company's space, you need to list both the customer group and the product category.

3. **Customer group.** Define your customer group by at least one and preferably two qualities. For example, young males interested in extreme sports, people interested in faux painting of their home, or people who keep koi (goldfish) in ponds in their backyards. The customer group is one of the most important points in a plan, because it's key to determining whether or not your business concept is good.

4. **Customer need or desire.** To succeed, a company needs a strong reason for customers to buy its product. That reason is typically based on the customers' needs or desires much more than on lower prices, better features, or better aesthetics. You want to show that customers are motivated to buy your product.

5. **Market size.** Great customers with a strong desire to buy in a big market. What could be better? Not very much. The actual size of the market is not as important as its relationship to a company's goals. I've found an ideal market size is between 10 and 20 percent of your eventual business goals. For example, if you want to be one of the top restaurants in Northeast Cincinnati, you might want to define your geographic area to include 5 to 10 other top restaurants in the area. Most companies have trouble gaining more than 20 percent market share—competition is just too fierce. If you aim for less than 10 percent market share, you will have trouble being noticed in the market.

6. **Goals.** You will list sales goals and history at the end of the summary as numbers, but I feel you should state your market share goal right after market size. Clearly define your market in terms of customer group, application or market segment, and, if relevant, geographic area.

7. **Key advantage.** The important point in the executive summary is that you have a lucrative customer group. You only have to mention briefly in the summary that you have a competitive advantage. Too often plans try to

explain that advantage in detail in the summary. If people want to know more, they'll read it in a following section in the plan. The key in the summary is to list the advantage in a short phrase that's easy to remember. For example, Guitarland has twice the inventory of its competitors, XYZ's patented technology is three times as effective as the competition, and Freight Tomorrow has the most extensive fulfillment facility in the Denver area. Simple statements like this will show you are not a "me-too" company.

Pitfalls to Avoid

Business owners and marketers know their product, service, and market backwards and forwards. They often try to impress the readers of their business plan with their expertise. Unfortunately, people understand less and less of your business concept as you increase the technical content of your plan. If you are working to raise money or get a loan, concentrate on making your business easy to understand.

8. **Timing.** In some cases timing is critical, such as new retail businesses in a growing neighborhood, a new type of service business, or the introduction of a new product for a new application. If timing is critical, especially in the case of changes in the market, explain why.

9. **Management.** This is key to any successful business. You will have trouble getting money even with a great business model if you don't have a strong management team. If there are just one or two managers or if your experience is light, you need to have a team of advisors with lots of experience in your industry. I've found it worthwhile to give up equity if necessary to attract the type of managers who will make your venture grow. The most important feature in the summary is past business experience with relevant companies.

10. **Operations.** This section would mention manufacturing facilities, administration, and other business functions. This normally isn't included in the summary unless the company's operations offer it a unique advantage in the market.

11. **Sales history/projections/margins.** This section typically gives sales, if any, for the last two years and projections for the next three years. It's also appropriate to list the margins you expect each year. Some people will also list the income per year.

This section is often presented in whatever format shows the company in the most positive light. Income is left off if a company is losing money. Only the prior year's sales are shown if sales have not been growing. Future sales need to be realistic in the first year of the plan; after that they can grow.

Business plans tend to project the future in dramatically different ways depending on the objective. Businesses that are looking for investors often show sales doubling or even tripling every year. Investors want to see the business growing rapidly, even if to grow it has to spend all of its profits on sales and marketing activities. A business plan oriented toward getting money from a banker will be more conservative, showing profits much sooner and showing that money invested will be going toward tangible assets such as equipment and inventory.

Success Tip

I've consulted for many companies where employees think the sales numbers in a plan are smoke and mirrors for investors. This is a dangerous situation, as investors and bankers will eventually talk with some of those employees and it won't take them long to see that employees don't believe the numbers. Before you finalize the plan, be sure your staff buys into your growth for the future.

12. **Capitalization or financing plan.** This section should be included any time you are selling stock or borrowing money. If you are not borrowing or raising money, you can leave this section out.

If you're approaching investors or a bank, always start this section by stating how much money you are raising or borrowing. *Capitalization* is a statement of what a company is worth. It's calculated by multiplying the number of shares that are owned in the company by the price you're currently charging for buying shares. Investors also want to see how much of the company is being bought in the current round of funding. For capitalization, list the number of shares currently owned and the number you're trying to sell. You may also be borrowing money for your business. You would want to list here the sources of the money: for example, a percentage from your resources, a percentage from vendors, and a percentage from a bank.

Sample Section—PlayBoxes Etc., Inc.

Executive Summary

Company Description

PlayBoxes Etc., Inc. markets old-fashioned playboxes including dress-up kits and conversion kits for boxes, turning them into castles or playhouses. The playboxes foster unstructured creativity in young children and are meant as a counter to the structured interactivity of computer games and "educational" TV. Products are sold through retailers and on a peer-produced web site for parents interested in fostering creativity in their children.

Opportunity

Two target customer groups are the parents and grandparents of young children with parental income of over $70,000 (approximate market size 4,225,000), and preschool and education centers (approximate market size 135,000 centers). There has been a boom in the last few years in structured interactive toys, including software and handheld games for young children. A backlash is building that children need to be able to create their own fun to foster creativity, and that structured interactive toys take away from children's ability to be creative. Internet sites like www.childparentingabout.com, www.thingamababy.com, www.oldfashionliving.com, and www.oldfashionblocks.com all promote the value of old-fashioned toys where children receive little structure and devise their own games and rules. While old-fashioned toys never disappeared, their influence has waned and now is an ideal time to lead the way with playboxes and other creative toys for young children. Each playbox also comes with helpful hints for parents to assist in fostering their child's creativity.

Success Tip

This plan combines information on its target customer (parents and educational centers), the customers' needs (helpful tools for generating creativity in young children), the market size (a large number of parents and educational centers), and company goals (offering creative toys for young children), into one section called Opportunity. "Opportunity" is a positive term and more interesting than section headings like "Customer Group" and "Customer Need." Remember that your business plan is in most cases an effort to sell your company.

Products

The company primarily sells playboxes, which include some items for the children to play with, instructions on other items parents can create to add to the playbox, and simple instructions for the parents to help the child get started.

Playboxes include:

- Medieval Castles and Knights
- Construction Crew
- Kitchen Helper
- Clay Studio
- Star Searcher
- Big Box Conversions
- Cereal Box Construction Kits
- Wild Animal Babies

Management

Steve Kellar, company cofounder and president. Experience includes three years as a second-grade teacher, four years as manager of a Zany Brainy, and then five years as a manufacturer's representative of educational toys such as GuideCraft, Chicco, Rock-N-Learn, and Munchkin.

Heather Navarro, company cofounder, product creator, and director of product development. Heather, a mother of three small children, was creating and selling playboxes at children's expos, state, and county fairs, as well as selling to several local retails before launching PlayBoxes Etc. to create a nationwide market.

Olivia Spader, administrative officer. Experience includes three years as controller of Harmony Outdoor Furniture, and four years as purchasing agent and accountant at Sunrise Products.

Goals

1. $300,000 in revenue for the year starting January 1, 2007
2. Have five representative groups ready to sell to toy stores by January 1, 2007
3. Have five representative groups ready to sell to children's centers by January 1, 2007
4. Have fully operational peer-produced Web site by July 1, 2007
5. Raise $200,000 in private investments by January 1, 2007

Financial Summary

Year	Sales	Profit
2007	$300,000	−$6,000
2008	$920,000	$61,000
2009	$1,530,000	$212,000
2010	$2,240,000	$431,000

Capitalization	Percent ownership
Current Shares—360,000	60%
Shares offered at $1 per share—240,000	40%
Total shares after investments—200,000	100%

Success Tip

Most new businesses set the price of stock on their first investment go-around at 50 cents to $1 per share. One of the sales points given to early investors is that they are getting in cheap, that the stock will be more expensive on future rounds of fundraising. In other words, you're saying, "Buy now because the stock is cheap." The sales price of 50 cents to a dollar reinforces that image.

Chapter 12

Overview

Thecolumn **T**HE BUSINESS PLAN IS CONSTANTLY SELLING THE CONCEPT OF A unique opportunity. The obvious place to do this is when you describe your product or service and its proprietary features. But I think a more important place to emphasize the uniqueness is in telling how the business comes together.

For example, a technology company stated in its overview that it was an offshoot of an organization that had 200 computer programmers. That implies plenty of programming power. A company that sold medical products included in its overview the story of how the product was invented by an operating room nurse and was then immediately purchased by four area hospitals. Better yet are stories of companies where the idea sat and percolated until the right management team came together. You should try to make this section of the plan a story that explains why the owners found starting a company so compelling.

The purpose of this section is to show that your business makes lots of sense and that you only went into business after careful thought and a considerable amount of research. This is the part of the plan where you show people just how seriously you approached going into business. The overview is really just a capsule view of why you went into business and what your business has done to date. If you've been in business for a while, you want

---

Success Tip

How carefully will you be running your business? Well, people can't really tell, but one of the ways they judge you is by how carefully you've moved with your company till the timeframe of your plan. Spend a little extra time in the overview to demonstrate that you are a thoughtful businessperson. I've found people's confidence in entrepreneurs is often related to how well they present the beginnings of their business.

---

this section to show how you've positioned your business in the past, what changes you've made, and how you've set the stage for your future moves.

What to Communicate

1. That you founded this business because of a real and significant opportunity.
2. That you've carefully looked into this opportunity before moving ahead. I believe it's worthwhile to include a few interviews with real customers in this section about the market opportunity.
3. That you've assembled the people and resources and connections to move forward on this opportunity. Even if the people are mentors or just offering advice, list the industry people who have encouraged you to move ahead.
4. Perhaps most importantly, that you have assembled or have access to people experienced in the market and industry that you're targeting.

Format

1. **Describe your business.** Include the following information in your plan:
   - the business structure, e.g., a sole proprietorship or partnership
   - the type of business, e.g., a retail store, an Internet seller, a manufacturer, or a service company
   - how you produce income—your product or service
   - your target customers
   - your market
   - how your product is distributed
   - how you make your product or provide your service

Pitfalls to Avoid

Business plans too often read like a business or market research report. But investors, banks, and even employees want to see commitment or a passion that will carry forth even when things aren't going well. Sometimes that passion is evident from the time you've invested in your business already or from past activities related to your business. Don't be afraid to express why your business is more than just a job.

2. **Explain your company's background.** This should be a story about why you and the other founders thought this was a great business opportunity to explore or what was so intriguing about the idea that got you started. I've found over the years that most entrepreneurs have an exceptionally strong reason for going into business, something that impressed them and gave them the fire inside that they needed to get their idea to the market. You need to convey that passion or strong reason here.

3. **List any significant events that have occurred.** This is actually a part of the company's history, but I like to include a special section to highlight any points I feel are of particular interest. This tactic is particularly important if you want to raise money from investors, because many of them will skim the plan. A "significant events" section will typically catch their attention.

4. **Explain your company's current status.** You need to tell exactly where you are. I've found that investors and other plan readers get irritated when entrepreneurs sugar-coat the company's current status too much. If it's bad, state why it's bad—and then say why the situation has turned around. I've found that both investors and banks expect entrepreneurs to encounter troubles. It doesn't bother them as long as the entrepreneurs deal with the problems. Hiding from the problems is the worst-case scenario.

5. **Outline your future plans for the company.** Many plans like to list a vision or a mission here, but those statements usually are idealistic and don't really offer much insight into how the company is going to evolve. In this section, you should talk about how you will grow your business from its current levels. You shouldn't worry about whether you have the money now to reach those levels, only that this is where your business could go if everything works out right. This is especially true if you need investors, who will usually look for businesses with growth rates of over 100 percent per year.

> ## Pitfalls to Avoid
>
> You're obviously in business because you think you have a great business concept. Don't sell your concept short by being too conservative when talking about your future growth. People expect entrepreneurs to oversell their potential a little bit, so they'll feel you don't have a passion for your business if you're too conservative.

Sample Section—PlayBoxes Etc., Inc.

Overview

Company Description

PlayBoxes Etc. is an LLC that provides playboxes with dress-up clothes, props, and kits for converting boxes and other household items. The kits allow young children to use their imagination to create their own play environment. The products are aimed at parents of young children and children's educational centers who want to offer the old-fashioned play environment to their children because it is less structured and allows more creativity. The company plans on selling its products through two sales rep organizations, one that sells to retail stores and the other that sells to young children's care and educational centers.

The company is coordinating a peer-produced web site regarding creative play with two mothers of young children, who knew cofounder Heather Navarro, and who have been involved with creating and maintaining web sites for consumer products. They have agreed to produce, monitor, and maintain the site in return for 50 percent of the site-generated revenue.

History

Steve Kellar and Heather Navarro created PlayBoxes in 2005. Heather is a mother of three young children who was not willing to immerse her young children in computer games and TV. She had loved play acting as a child and created several playboxes for her children. When her friends liked the idea and started making their own "dress up" boxes, she decided to make her own line of playboxes to sell. Beginning in 2003 she sold playboxes at Early Family Childhood Education fairs around Minnesota and at some local fairs. Navarro sold $25,000 in product in the two years before launching PlayBoxes Etc.

At the Minnesota State Fair in 2005 Steve Kellar saw Navarro's products. He had a background in educational stores, being manager of a Zainy Brainy and then a manufacturer's sales rep for various toy companies.

Customer Need

Jean Piaget and Mark Edwards, two of the prime sources for educational development of young children, both support dramatic play as a key element in a young child's development. "Dramatic play permits children to fit the reality of the world into their own interests and knowledge. One of the purest forms of symbolic thought available to young children, dramatic play contributes strongly to the intellectual development of children" (Piaget, 1962). "Symbolic play is a necessary part of a child's language development" (Edwards, 1976).

While toddlers and young children are being exposed to computers and computer educational software, there is still a strong demand for old-fashioned playboxes. Just one of a recent magazine quotes include: "One of the best ways children have to express themselves is through creative dramatic play. Here they feel free to express their inner feelings. It occurs daily in the lives of young children, as they constantly imitate the people, animals, and machines in their world. It helps them understand and deal with the world. Stimulate this spontaneous kind of drama by providing simple props and encouragement." (National Network of Childcare, Marilyn Lopes, University of Massachusetts).

The demand for dramatic play from early childhood educators should help fuel a demand for playboxes from parents, and together they present a strong opportunity for PlayBoxes Etc., who will be able to take a leadership role as this market re-emerges.

Current Status

The company has conducted research with Kellar's industry contacts at both retailers and rep organizations and after receiving positive feedback, the Kellar and Navarro team launched PlayBoxes Etc. To date the company has worked with a retailer and one rep group to repackage the products so they are ready for retail stores and created books and guides for each product so parents and educators can supplement the playboxes with additional home-made props and activities. The product line has been shown to 12 Midwest stores and five are ready to place orders. The company is now seeking funding to cover its cost for an initial production run.

Future Plans

PlayBoxes Etc.'s plan is to first sell to individual stores that foster children's creativity and to educational centers for young children that believe in the benefits of dramatic play. Once established in those markets, the company plans on branching out to partnership arrangements with leading childhood educational companies like Scholastic and major mass merchandisers such as Target, Wal-Mart, and K-Mart. The company needs to build a solid base first with the organizations that are considered experts in creativity in order to create the "buzz" among parents that dramatic play is at a minimum a complementary tool to computers to foster creativity and, at best, the preferred route to a creative child.

Success Tip

A good plan should progress along with the company's financial and management capability. PlayBoxes Etc.'s management has deep experience with representative groups, independent stores, and childhood educational centers. Investors and bankers like to see the company concentrating first on areas where it is strong to build a base of profitable business before it strikes out into markets that are more difficult to enter and/or markets where the management has limited experience.

Chapter 13

Target Customers and Markets

MANY COMPANIES PUT A COMPANY DESCRIPTION AFTER THE EXEC-utive summary. My experience is that people either don't read or don't understand the company description if it is placed here. Instead, I prefer to place the description in the "Company Operations" section, which comes after you explain your customers, products, markets, competitive advantages, and marketing strategy.

This section of the plan should explain the customer group you're targeting and the market that you are focusing on. The customers and market are tied together. For example, Amazon's target customers are people who buy lots of books and its market is Internet book sales. Amazon's customers may buy from other booksellers, such as direct sales or retail stores, and those markets compete with the Internet book market, but Amazon isn't in those markets.

What to Communicate

1. You have identified and can narrowly define a target customer group. One of the words you hear in this context all the time, from investors and bankers, is *focus*. You want to show not only that you know your

> ## Success Tip
>
> You need to be specific when defining a customer group. You don't want to simply state that you sell products to "manufacturers." It's better to put "manufacturers with machine shops"; better yet to add "that have a lot of CNC milling machines"; and even better to add "that machine stainless steel." The more narrowly you define your customer group, the easier it is to determine the customers' needs.

target customer group but also that you have built your business around their needs and desires.

2. The target customer group is large, easy to find, and free spending. Of course, most businesses don't have such a dream customer group, but you want to show that your customer group is one that will be receptive to your product.

3. Customers have a need or desire that you will fulfill. You want to show that you offer something that the customers need or desire and you want to explain why they need or desire it.

4. The market is well-defined, easy to penetrate, not overcrowded, and reached through defined distribution channels. You'll find that most investors and banks steer away from new market channels until they are proven. The Internet, for example, existed for about 10 years before it became the "hot new market." New markets are full of question marks and danger.

Format

I recommend you have three main headings in this section: Customers, Opportunity, and Market. You may want to add a special section if it enhances your plan and possible business success. You want to be sure to cover the following points.

1. **Customers—characteristics.** Describe the group and some of their characteristics as they are relevant to your business. Don't get carried away in this part, just give enough information to let the reader understand who the customer is.

2. **Customers—numbers.** If possible, give the number of customers or otherwise show that there are enough customers to support your business.

3. **Customers—facts.** You want to show that you've researched your customers and understand them well. You don't want to burden the reader

Pitfalls to Avoid

Customers and their behavior are not easy to understand. I've found that one of the major flaws in many businesses is that the company doesn't really understand their customer. The best way to demonstrate that you know customers is if you and some of your managers are members of the customer group or if one of your managers has successfully sold to the group at another company.

with facts here, but you must show more than just library research. You need to demonstrate an "industry insider" understanding of the customer. Present facts here, though, only if they're relevant to your business concept.

4. **Customers—how they can be reached or identified.** Include this information if it's not obvious how you'll find customers. In many cases, businesses don't have trouble identifying customers and you don't need to include this part. But in other cases, identifying them can be quite a problem. For example, how do you identify companies that are in the market for an e-procurement system?

5. **Opportunity—what is the need or desire?** You need to explain why customers are going to be motivated to buy your product or service. The answer is never that your product or service is great with tons of benefits. The answer is always that the customers are buying for their agenda—whether emotion, ego, functionality, or desire to please others.

6. **Opportunity—why the need or desire is important.** How can you prove that something is important? I've found that the best way is to demonstrate what people are doing already to meet this need or desire. What other products or services are they buying or what steps are they taking in their life to meet this need or satisfy this desire? The greater the effort they make, the more important the need or desire is to them.

7. **Opportunity—the choices.** You should list other ways people could or are meeting this need or desire. You want to list direct competitors, if you have any, or indirect competitors, which are different products people buy to meet the same need. For example, wallpaper or regular painting would be substitutes or indirect competitors for faux painting.

8. **Opportunity—the reason other choices aren't working.** The easiest products or services to sell are ones that compete against products or services that just don't work well enough. It's ideal if your product or service corrects a big problem. You might also have a product that improves a

---

Success Tip

Make sure that your plan states that there's a dramatic opportunity for your product. People have to need or desire it. For example, When Ford introduced its Expedition sports utility vehicle (SUV), it made sure it was dramatically bigger than the Jeep Cherokee. The SUV that the Expedition replaced was the Explorer, which was the same size as the Cherokee. "Dramatic" means your product is at least 20 percent better than other products.

---

product drawback for one segment of the market or a product that offers significantly better benefits than current products.

9. **Market—definition and size.** Define the market and estimate its size. The market is where you do business. This can be defined by a geographic area, type of customers, and type of product. For a retail store, the market is a geographic area and a type of product. A paint store's market, for instance, would be the retail paint market in the western suburbs. For a manufacturer to businesses, the market is often the product category, price range, or performance characteristic of the product and a type of customer. For example, a company that sells satellite communication systems to truckers might have as its market high-end communication systems for over-the-road trucking firms. A service company would define its market by type of customer and service, such as marketing consultant to emerging companies.

The size of the market should be defined in terms of the geographic area you serve and/or type of customers you serve. If you are currently serving a small segment of the market, for example, Chicago, but have long-term plans to serve a bigger market, you can list both the immediate market and the future market.

10. **Market—competition.** Who are the competitors and what are their strengths and weaknesses? Don't go into too much detail here about products that directly compete with yours; you should cover that in the Product section (Chapter 14). You want instead to focus on methods other than your type of product or service that people might use to meet the same need or desire that your product or concept meets. For example, a coffee house with evening entertainment might compete with a coffee bar, restaurants with a piano, or intimate clubs.

11. **Market—distribution, number of channels, and how they work.** A distribution channel is the method by which a product or service moves from your company to the point where the customer can buy it. In the case of

> ## Pitfall to Avoid
>
> If you ask investors, "What is the most important factor in marketing?" they will probably answer, "Distribution." Yet I consistently find plans that underestimate the difficulty of setting up distribution or, even worse, ignore distribution altogether. This is especially true if you're selling to retailers or businesses. It's also true for service businesses. Include in your strategy a way for getting your product in front of customers so they can buy.

a service company, distribution could be that you have a telemarketing sales force, a direct sales force, a marketing arrangement with another company, or an arrangement with independent sales representatives. A retail store's distribution includes its location, since that's the vehicle that brings products to the customer. But distribution could also include selling at shows, from a catalog, or through a direct sales force. For a manufacturer of hammers, for example, the channel might be general hardware distributors, specialty distributors selling to home improvement chains, or a network of manufacturers' sales agents that sell to union carpenters.

Sample Section—PlayBoxes Etc.

Target Customers and Markets

Target Customers—Consumers

This segment includes people buying a single product for their children or someone they know. The demographics of this segment are a household income of greater than $50,000 with high aspirations for their children in terms of education and development and a desire to start helping their children. Generally the group will have an undergraduate degree with 41 percent of the segment having a graduate degree.

According to Simmons, a leading market research firm in the toy industry, 14.6 million U.S. households, or 13.2 percent of the total population, bought infant toys and games in 2005 and more than 13.1 million households bought preschool toys or games. According to the Bureau of Census, the population of children under age 1 will increase by 5.7 percent to over 4.1 million, while kids aged 1 to 5 will increase 4 percent to 19.9 million between 2005 and 2010.

Playboxes fit into the educational toy category, which is a rapidly increasing category, due in part to the increasing number of older first-time parents in their thirties and even forties, who are well-educated and primed to foster creativity in children. A recent survey at the 2006 Toy Stores found that 535 of retailers selling toys listed educational toys as an important category. That was the highest listed category of over 20 possibilities.

Target Customers—Preschools and Educational Centers

This group buys toys and educational games for children who are the businesses' clients. These organizations are either day care–based or school-based such as a nursery school or preschool. The number of children they care for ranges from 7 to 25.

Potential customers for 2006 are approximately 135,000, with a 7 to 10 percent growth rate forecasted. Playboxes have long been a favorite of early childhood educators, and early conversations with sales groups serving this market indicate that the market will be willing to purchase PlayBoxes Etc.'s product line.

Success Tip

The customer group is, as discussed in the GEL factor analysis, probably the key element in the success of every business. Make sure your plan focuses on a customer group that is easy to understand. This is not a problem with PlayBoxes Etc., but other customer groups are more difficult. For example, having your target customers as businesses trying to reach males 18 to 27 is hazy. You need to define the category more finely, such as saying the target customers are marketers trying to reach young males, with a special emphasis on travel destinations and chain restaurants, and a second target market of banks and insurance companies. Those are customer groups with more clarity that people can understand.

Customer Need

Dress-up, dramatic play, and make believe are flying in the face of computer games, educational software, and educational TV, all noninteractive toys that have grown rapidly in the market. While books [by leading lecturers, opposing the trend to noninteractive play, such as James Healey's *Failure to Connect: How Computers Affect Our Children's Minds and What we Can Do about It* (Broadway, 3d ed., 2004) and Vivian Gussin Paley's *A Child's Work: The Importance of Fantasy Play* (University of Chicago Press, 2004)], have developed a following, the clearest sign that parents recognize the value of dramatic play is the rapid growth of children's museums, where dramatic play and the playbox concepts dominate.

The first children's museum opened in 1899 in Brooklyn, but early museums were primarily a collection of dolls, trains, and other toys on display. In the 1960s the Boston Children's Museum opened the first interactive exhibit and since then children's museums has been on a rapid growth curve. There were 35 children's museums in 1975, 80 more opened between 1976 and 1990, and another 100 have opened since (Association of Children's Museums).

The web page of the Habitot Children's Museum, www.habitot.org/hab/mission.htm, lists its core values, which capture the same spirit that Play-Boxes Etc. strives to achieve. Two of those values are:

▶ Creativity, discovery and curiosity are cultivated through hands-on exhibits and programs which foster a passion for lifelong learning.

▶ Our goal is to help all young children reach their potential—by interacting with engaging, hands-on exhibits, and by experiencing creative programs.

Pitfall to Avoid

Don't assume your readers will believe you are an expert on your market or your customers. List references, quotes from experts, and other source material to prove your point. The best information to include is quotes from interviews or other research you've conducted with end users. Every business plan is stronger with some feedback from customers—why they used the product or service, and how much they liked the product or service.

Industry Analysis

Total toy sales (including educational toys) to toddlers and preschoolers were $4.1 billion in 2005 and are expected to grow to $5.2 billion in the 2005–2010 period. Sixty-six percent of the toys are sold through mass merchandisers and 30 percent through specialty retailers such as Toys 'R Us and K-B Toys (*Souvenirs, Gifts and Novelties* Magazine, February 2006).

An article in the February 2006 *Souvenirs, Gifts and Novelties* magazine describes the favorable trends for new entrees into the young children toy industry. "As American parenting continues to become more and more sophisticated, the demand for ITP (infant, toddler, and preschool) toys will only become greater and greater. The ongoing trend has been widely observed, but is difficult to quantify; perhaps the best proof is in the various toy companies' own product catalogs, in which educational toys now comprise key collections within a broader line. Moreover, there are many companies that have been created by entrepreneurs wholly to bank on the need for educational toys, and some of these fairly new companies are major success stories. The prime example is LeapFrog Enterprises, Inc., based in Emeryville, California. Established in 1995 specifically to create educational, mostly electronic and interactive toys, the company reported sales of $640 million in 2004."

Competition

While there are other companies that produce costumes and other variations of playboxes, there are not many other choices for creative and dramatic play. The largest competitor is parents who make their own costumes and design their own dramatic play areas. PlayBoxes Etc. encourages parents to have an area in their home set aside for dramatic play, and its products are designed to either help parents start a dramatic play area, or to augment the dramatic play areas that parents or schools have started. (See section on dramatic play dress-up products.)

Distribution

The retail industry sales are 66 percent through mass merchandisers and 30 percent to specialty retailers. Catalogs are the other main distribution outlet. Mass merchandisers are typically sold direct by the manufacturer, but mass merchandisers are typically reluctant to start buying from a small company without an established sales history. Specialty retailers, especially small retail chains, will buy from smaller manufacturers, and often buy from manufacturers' sales representatives that sell products from a number of toy manufacturers. Children's educational centers are sold either direct, primarily from trade show attendance, or through manufacturers' sales representatives.

PlayBoxes Etc.'s plan is to establish its presence in the specialty and educational markets in the first four years and then branch out into the mass merchandisers once the company has built up a financial base and established market presence. The company cofounder, Steve Kellar, has extensive contacts in the toy industry's manufacturers' sales representative network and has already located five representative groups in each market with a strong interest in carrying PlayBoxes Etc. products.

Pitfall to Avoid

Companies with the distribution network in many industries act as the gate-keepers, or the companies or individuals that block many companies' entry into the market. Many times you can't get your product to retailers until you first sell it to distributors. They are often the hardest sale a new marketer will face. Distributors may even balk at taking on a new product when a marketer has retailers lined up to sell your product. If applicable to your company, take the time in your plan to clearly indicate that you have a plan to create your own distribution network and emphasize that you can create your network right when you have product available.

Chapter 14

Your Product and Your Advantage

YOUR PRODUCT IS WHATEVER YOU ARE SELLING: IT DOESN'T MATTER if it's a service, a monthly maintenance, or a physical product people can touch and feel. If you have a retail store, your product is really the concept of the store and your merchandise, service, and your layout. Features, which typically produce your advantage, are the aspects of your product or service that offer benefits to customers. For example, Home Depot's concept, or product, is a big home improvement store with plenty of expert assistance on "how-to" projects. Home Depot's prices, product selection, and location are all features of the stores.

In some cases, companies have a new technology that generates new products. If your technology is different, you should also have a section in the plan that discusses what your technology is, why it's better, and how you know it will work. New technology is a double-edged sword as far as investors are concerned. On the one hand, it offers the possibility of significant patent protection and a leading-edge position that could dominate the market. On the other hand, new technology rarely works as well as people anticipate, it often takes much longer to perfect than anyone expects, and it often has unexpected developments that kill the project.

Pitfalls to Avoid

Entrepreneurs often take space in their plans talking about how great a technology is or how strong a patent is. Investors and banks are worried about whether a product will sell. The strength of a technology is not as important as how you've positioned a product for sales. If you talk too much about technology, investors might believe that you feel your product "will sell itself"—something that rarely, if ever, happens.

I recommend you include your new technology as part of your Product section. The emphasis of a plan needs to be on the customers and why the customers will want to buy your product. In this section, you need to explain what your product is, how it relates to the customers' needs and desires, its pricing, its benefits, and how it compares to competition. You need to be careful not to give too much detail in this segment, for example, listing the product's 12 top features, as that will give the impression that your product is too complex and difficult to understand, which means that it will be hard to sell. Think instead of the one or two overriding reasons that a customer will buy your product and keep the focus of the section on those two points.

What to Communicate

1. **That your product is easy for customers to understand.** Prospective customers should be able to understand your product in less than 10 seconds, which means that you should be able to describe it in fewer than 30 words. I believe this is absolutely necessary for a business plan, especially if you are raising money. If at all possible, try to show how your product's look or your company's logo and slogans help customers immediately understand what your product is and why it's better.

2. **That your product has an outstanding benefit that will make it easy to sell.** A key question any investor or banker asks about a business plan is "Will customers buy?" The best answer to this question is that you already have lots of customers buying. But in lieu of that, the best solution is to simply have a benefit that's clearly superior to anything competitors have.

3. **That if your product sells through distribution, your product meets the requirements of the distribution channel.** Distribution channels are your first customer and you need to be sure you meet their requirements,

> ## Pitfall to Avoid
>
> Many business plans take the approach that there's simply no positive sales point that should be left unmentioned. All that does is make the plan too long, too wordy, and in the end very forgettable. People remember only two or three points, so make those points strong. And then don't dilute your strong points by listing weaker benefits.

which could mean going on peg board hooks, or fitting onto a shelf of a specific size, or being in the right price range for an upscale store. If you don't have actual job experience in your market, be sure to have an advisor who gives you the exact requirements of the channel.

4. **That your product concept is new or different in your target market.** You want to position your product as more than just another "me-too" entry into the market, but instead a new concept that better meets customers' needs and desires.

5. **That your product has significantly better benefits than competing products.** Your uniqueness isn't worth much if it doesn't translate into improved customer benefit(s). Hopefully, the benefit is 20 to 30 percent better than what the competition offers.

6. **That your product is strong enough to build a growing business in the future.** You want to convince investors and bankers that you're in business for the long haul. To do that, you need to show that your product line can be naturally expanded in the future to better meet the needs of your current customers or of new customer groups, so that your business can grow.

Format

1. **Describe your product line or set of services.** You may have several products or services, or in the case of a store, many departments. You need to list all of these services, but in a way that enforces that you are concentrating on one customer group or one market. The ideal product line is one where each product adds to the others. For example, Claire's Boutique stores have several departments, including jewelry, cosmetics, and hair products, but they are all aimed at preteen and teenaged girls. The lines reinforce each other and add to the Claire Boutique credibility.

2. **Key benefits.** List here the three main customer benefits of your product or service. These benefits should directly tie back to the customer needs or desires in your Customers section.

Success Tip

Write your plan as if your readers know little about your industry. Don't use lots of acronyms without explaining what they mean and don't assume that readers will understand the functions of your features. Ask someone unfamiliar with your business to read the plan's Product section and then see if he or she can explain what your product does. Cut back on industry jargon so that any reader can understand your product.

3. **The overriding reason customers will buy.** In some cases, companies will have an exceptionally strong reason people will buy. Take the PT Cruiser, for example: the look—something different, something for the young—is the overwhelming reason for its success.

4. **Distribution channel requirements.** Distribution concerns don't exist with every product, but if your product will eventually end up on retailers' shelves, be sure to explain the criteria of the distribution channel(s) and how you meet them. You only want to cover the major requirements of distribution, which includes product packaging, discount terms, and marketing support.

5. **Show that you are better than your competition.** Don't go into too much depth on competitors, because you really want to sell your concept as unique. Dwelling on competition just seems to tell people that you aren't really that different. The only time I recommend you offer more than a paragraph or two on competition is when there are one or two dominant companies in the market. You need to be clear explaining why you have an opening to compete against those companies. You either need to have a feature or benefit that they don't have or you need a product that performs significantly better for one segment of the market.

6. **Your long-term future.** The best way to demonstrate this is to show that your product or service is just the first step in satisfying the needs of your target customer group. The next best tactic is to show that you will be able to take your products and services out to new markets. Investors particularly want you to demonstrate that you have a long-term vision for the company that will grow sales 5 to 10 times over the next few years.

Sample Section—PlayBoxes Etc., Inc.

Products

The company offers two categories of products, one is its actual product line of playboxes and the other is its Web site. The Web site, which is peer-produced and run by two stay-at-home moms, who each receive one-third of the revenue, is primarily meant to provide marketing support for PlayBoxes Etc.'s product line.

The playbox line of products all have a suggested retail price of $39.99, and include (1) three dress-up items, (2) a kit for converting a cardboard box or boxes into part of the play set, (3) a list of other items a parent can add to the playbox to increase the kit's creative play value, and (4) a booklet on how parents can get their children started on the play experience. All of the products are packaged in an 18-inch by 24-inch by 6-inch box and come with attractive packaging based on the company's retail store contacts.

Success Tip

Pricing can be confusing if you have a stream of products all with different prices, rather than just one standard product like PlayBoxes, Etc. If this is the case with your product, it is best to put your pricing in a table so it is easiest to see. Banks and investors also like to see gross margin percent for the product added to the chart. This is calculated using the following formula:

$$\frac{\text{Selling price} - \text{Cost to produce} \times 100\%}{\text{Selling price}}$$

Your margins should be at least 45 to 50 percent to impress investors.

The company will have the following kits available when the product line is launched.

▶ Medieval Castles and Knights: includes knight costumes, fabric to go on a hassock or other furniture for a horse, a kit to convert a large cardboard box into a castle, paper cut-outs for helmets, painting ideas for cardboard boxes, booklet of ideas on how to use the box, plus a list of movies that children might enjoy related to castles and knights.

▶ Construction Crew: includes helmet; road work vest; snap-together plastic for jackhammers, wrenches, drills, and toy hammer; instructions on making a tool holder out of a cardboard box, and other items parents can make at home; some suggestions on play; and a keep-out construction sign.

- ▶ Kitchen Helper: includes cooking bowls, mixing spatulas, cake pan, muffin tins, dishes, and a miniature apron, instructions on building a cardboard oven, children's cook book, cooking instructions, and a parent guide.

- ▶ Clay Studio: includes four boxes of clay, display trays, starting forms for special shapes, sculpting tools for children, picture book of shapes children can make, and a book for parents to help children get started.

Other products with similar contents will include: Star Searcher, Big Box Conversions, Cereal Box Construction Kits, and Wild Animal Babies.

The creative and dramatic play web site is listed as a product, as it will bring in advertising revenue and also be a vehicle for selling products direct to consumers. Its main purpose, though, is to be a community, peer-produced site for parents and educators of young children. Parents and educators can post their own advice for fostering creativity in children, advice that can be unrelated to the PlayBoxes Etc.'s product line. Two stay-at-home moms with backgrounds in technology have agreed to run the site in return for 50 percent of the advertising revenue and 20 percent of all product sales generated from the site. The peer-reviewed section will also encourage parents and educators to suggest new products, both playboxes and other products that can keep PlayBoxes Etc. on the leading edge.

Success Tip

What's too much and what's too little regarding details in the plan? A great deal depends on your situation. In the case of PlayBoxes Etc., the managers are not experienced and they need to convince readers that they have a very strong product line. So this plan spends extra time explaining PlayBoxes Etc.'s concept so that readers can develop confidence that the company will succeed. This product section is too long for a management team whose experience itself creates investor confidence.

Key Benefits

1. **Easy to understand product line** for parents looking for interactive dramatic play toys for their children.
2. **Price of $39.99 per kit is attractive** for retailers, parents, and childhood educational centers. Prices are comparable to kits that have costumes alone without the value-added features of Playboxes Etc.'s kits.
3. **Playboxes created to allow parents to easily add to the experience** with additional easy-to-make items from materials found around the house.

Pitfalls to Avoid

Make your benefit statements simple and clear-cut. Those are the points people can remember. PlayBoxes Etc.'s benefits are: they know dramatic play, they understand creativity, and they know how to get parents involved with improving their child's play. Those benefits are plenty strong and there isn't any need to go into greater depth than PlayBoxes Etc.'s plan.

4. **More complete product line gives PlayBoxes Etc. a big advantage** when selling to stores over the limited product line of competitors.
5. **Focus on dramatic play versus Halloween costumes is a big advantage** to parents and educators looking for a true dramatic play experience.

Competition

There are companies that offer dress-up kits and interactive play kits. Examples include Veterinarians Children's Costume, Role Playing Games, Harry Potter Costume Kits, Sleeping Beauty Kits, Cheerleader Kits, and Firefighter Children's Costume Kits. In addition, there are many companies that sell children's Halloween costumes. Most of these companies have a presence on the web and some of them have sales to independent children's educational toy stores. The majority of the industry is related to Halloween costumes and imitative play (mimicking an action hero like Harry Potter) rather than the free-form dramatic play promoted by PlayBoxes Etc.

Competitors for play kits include:

▶ Small Miracles, Inc.—sells primarily Halloween costumes for young girls.

▶ Rubies Costume Co. Inc.—sells licensed Halloween costumes, mostly of super heroes.

▶ The Good Knight Company—sells dramatic play toys for boys 5 to 8 years old related to knights, castles, and the medieval era.

▶ Fairy Finery Company—sells fairy costumes with some dramatic play accessories, but primarily focuses on birthday and Halloween costumes.

▶ Dynamic Design International—sells some dramatic play activities, but primarily a costume supplier.

▶ Brand New World—carries an extensive line of low-cost dramatic play costumes. Closest competitor to PlayBoxes Etc. Has a fine line of costumes but its products don't come with a complete kit that includes things parents can add, booklets on encouraging dramatic play, and interactive play advice relevant to the kit.

▶ Dress Up America Toy Incorporated—another close competitor similar to Brand New World with many costumes, some dramatic play characteristics, but lacking the complete kit approach of PlayBoxes Etc.

▶ Acting Out Products, Inc. Company—sells costumes with musical boxes and light-up boas for young girls so they can dance in their dramatic play. Products are more expensive and are not part of a complete kit.

Competitors for the dramatic play web site include:

▶ Dr. Toy.com, which is primarily a review site of available toys by one expert, Dr. Stevanne Auerbach (Dr. Toy). Does not include peer production but does have information such as Smart Play and Toys for a Lifetime to help guide parents to proper play activities.

Main Advantages

1. PlayBoxes Etc. products are different from competition because they encourage parents and educators to add to the kits and they also have books that encourage children to take their own lead rather than following a more structured role-playing game. The company's strategy takes the concept of play items in the market and packages them into an easy-to-use, consistent format for a broad product line.

2. The company's main emphasis to differentiate it from competition is by developing a following with teachers and parents with its peer-produced web site. And because it has Steve Kellar's better connections with the industry's manufacturers' representative network who can take the product into the broad market. They could quickly expost it to both specialized creative children toy retail stores and to early childhood educators.

Success Tip

"Main advantage" as used in this plan is a summary of points stated earlier. You should include a summary section on occasion, with a noticeable headline such as Main Advantage to catch the attention of people who are skimming your plan and not taking in all the information. They will see a section titled Main Advantage and realize this is a short section that they should read.

Chapter 15

Marketing Strategy

THE CLASSIC DEFINITION FOR A MARKETING STRATEGY INVOLVES THE Four Ps—*price, promotion, product,* and *placement,* with placement being another term for distribution. The product itself is covered in a separate section of the plan, which was discussed in Chapter 14. The classic definition, though, leaves out *positioning,* which is a term describing how you present your product to customers so that they connect with the product. For example, products might be positioned as low cost, for the youth market, or most dependable, rugged, adventuresome, or as the "in" thing to have. Price, promotion, product, and placement all work together to reinforce your positioning strategy, which is based on what your target customer group wants or needs and on how your product is different from what your competition is offering.

Once you decide on a positioning strategy and figure out how to reinforce that strategy with the features of the product, including price, and the type of ads and promotion you'll run, the next step is to decide your marketing strategy, which deals with how to reach customers—through advertising, trade shows, the Internet, and other means—and determines how to actually sell the product.

The goal of this section is simply to explain your marketing strategy and the tactics you'll use to implement it. The section is a little more detailed

Pitfall to Avoid

Most people assume they know all about marketing because they see advertising, they've attended trade shows, and people have sold them products. Those activities are only a part of marketing and they don't include positioning, which is the key to a successful campaign. Ignoring positioning in the plan will hurt your chances of attracting funding, as investors understand the crucial role it plays in a company's success.

than others in the plan because of the importance most investors or banks will place on marketing.

What to Communicate

1. That you understand that selling a product is never easy and that you have a comprehensive sales and marketing program.
2. That you are tapping into other resources through strategic alliances and/or distributors and sales agents to multiply the effectiveness of your marketing efforts.
3. That your marketing plan's focus is on your customers' needs and desires first and your product second. Your marketing strategy should show that it is geared to how customers buy, what they want to see, and how much support they need.
4. That you have several tactics for locating and then selling to customers. You need at least two to three approaches, especially if you are a new company, so that you have a better chance of finding a strategy that works effectively.
5. That you have developed an effective positioning strategy to help customers understand the benefits of your product or service.
6. That you have an aggressive marketing program to bring in sales. Sales don't just happen. If you expect sales results, you need an aggressive strategy.
7. That your marketing tactics are cost-effective and generate sales. If your company is new, you want to avoid tactics that may not have immediate sales results, such as being a minor sponsor at a trade show or meeting. Concentrate on efforts that will produce sales fast.

Success Tip

Investors and banks will be very skeptical that a new company will be able to make sales at anywhere near its projected rates. The two ways to get around this skepticism are first to have someone with experience in the market on your management team and second to have an established network of contacts who work for or with key potential customers. List your network of contacts in the Marketing section if you have any.

Format

1. **Explain your marketing objectives.** One of the purposes of a plan is for readers to see that you've thought out a plan and a strategy. They really can't tell how well you've designed your plan unless they know where you want to go. That's what your objectives tell them. Your objectives also give readers a chance to see that your strategy makes sense.

2. **Explain your positioning strategy;** how you're projecting your product, service, or company to the customer. Your strategy should clearly relate both to what your customers are looking for and to what your advantages are over competition. This statement should be strong enough to make prospects notice you.

3. **List your positioning tactics.** Now that you have a strategy, be sure to list how you will communicate it to customers. This can be in your pricing, your packaging, your ad strategy, your targeted distribution strategy, and any number of other ways, such as slogans, logos, and product design. List only three or five of your major positioning tactics or the section gets to be too long.

4. **List the major methods you will use to promote your company.** You want to illustrate three points here. The first is that there are easy-to-implement tactics available to you, such as major trade shows or associations, well-read trade magazines, or Internet portal sites targeting your audience. The second is that you have low-cost tactics available. For example, a golf product manufacturer might list as a tactic "advertising in major golf magazines." The problem is those ads cost $25,000 to $50,000 each. So the plan should also mention low-cost regional retailer shows that cost only a few thousand dollars to attend. The last key point is that there's a wide variety of tactics you can implement. That conveys the message that if one program doesn't work, there are many others that might.

Pitfalls to Avoid

Many new entrepreneurs put too much emphasis on advertising in their plans. Most advertising programs fail to cover their costs. I've seen some estimates that place the percentage of ads that fail between 80 and 90 percent. Your promotional program will make more sense to readers if it includes attendance at trade shows, seminars, contests, joint marketing efforts with other companies, and innovative uses of the Internet.

5. **Explain your distribution strategy.** This strategy explains how you're taking your product to end-user customers so they can buy it. It could be through a direct sales force, through a strategic alliance, through either your own catalog or other catalogs, through the location of a store, or through distributors. In reality, there are hundreds of ways to distribute a product. In this section you want to show that you are using established, easy-to-penetrate distribution networks.

6. **Present your sales strategy and your reasons for choosing it.** This section should focus on how you plan on selling your product or service to the people who'll pay you for it. So if you sell to distributors, the sales strategy should focus on how you will sell to those distributors. If you sell through an alliance, the sales strategy should focus on how the alliance will sell to the customers who pay you, with a lesser emphasis on how you will set up an alliance. Try to include as much face-to-face contact as you can in your strategy. You'll find that many readers, especially investors, will take a dim view of telemarketing as a sales strategy unless it's already the norm in the industry.

Section Sample—PlayBoxes Etc.

Marketing Strategy

Objectives

- ▶ Position the product line as an education-driven, proven tool for helping children develop creativity through dramatic play.
- ▶ Brand the PlayBoxes Etc. concept through uniform-looking packaging, packing size, and material contents.
- ▶ Create a network of five representatives each for the independent children's toy store and the young children educational market.

► Build awareness for the peer-produced web site with both parents and young children educators interested in dramatic play. The company expects the web site to break even.

> ## Success Tip
>
> Objectives need to be obtainable, specific, and at least somewhat measurable. PlayBoxes Etc.'s objectives are straightforward and not all that dramatic, which is how they should be. If you set your objectives too high, readers might feel that you have a "pie in the sky" approach that is due to fail. While PlayBoxes Etc.'s objectives may not be glamorous, readers will still realize achieving its goals will be a challenge.

Positioning Statement

PlayBoxes Etc.'s product line is educator-prepared playboxes to enhance dramatic play for young children, that also encourage active parent participation.

Positioning Tactics

► Creation of the PlayBoxes Etc. web site as a peer-produced community web site promoting the concept of dramatic play.

► Packaging will reinforce that Playbox Etc.'s product line is produced by experienced educators.

► The booklets, list of extra props, and auxiliary items that can be added are all called Parent Helpers, to help encourage parent involvement.

► Participation in National Association for the Education of Young Children (NAEYC) and similar groups to align PlayBoxes Etc.'s product line, in both the eyes of customers and in reality, with the latest developments regarding dramatic play.

Pricing

Pricing in the market ranges from low-end Halloween costumes at $9.99 to high-end play kits and costumes that can run over $100. PlayBoxes Etc. has set its price at $39.99, which is at the lower end of the top-end pricing for the following reasons:

► Pricing to emphasize the toy is educator-developed and to sell the value of the Parent Helper aids included in every product.

► Comparable pricing to other premium toys such as bigger Lego or

163

Lincoln Log kits, and still below the price of educational software toys such as Leap Frog.

- ► Offer a price that will encourage parents and grandparents to buy four to five kits.
- ► Offer a price that is on the lower end of what young children educational centers pay for creative toys.

Pitfalls to Avoid

Don't shortchange your information on pricing and how you use your pricing to help position your product in the consumer's eye. Be careful though if you say that your product is being priced high to give your concept a premium image. That image must be created by offering a premium product or service, and the image can then be reinforced with the right price. Pricing alone can't create a premium image.

Promotional Tactics

- ► Promote and brand the PlayBoxes Etc. name and products through the peer-produced web site, trade links to other sites, and contributions to dramatic play articles to other sites.
- ► Attend National Association for the Education of Young Children (NAEYC) conventions.
- ► Attend local Children's Expos in areas where the company has local sales representatives.
- ► Run an active press release program to both educator magazines and local newspaper sections related to children, emphasizing both dramatic play and new product announcements.

Success Tip

If you need a plan to raise money, a good rule is to know what investors' perceptions are of various tactics. PlayBoxes Etc.'s plan talks about having a peer-produced community web site. Peer-produced web sites include Wikipedia, the much discussed online enclyopedia, and the very profitable community site, iVillage. PlayBoxes Etc.'s Internet site creates investor confidence by offering two features that are well received by the market: a community site and a peer-produced site.

Distribution Strategy

PlayBoxes Etc.'s distribution strategy is to sell to parents and grandparents through specialty children's retail stores and to young children educators through manufacturers' sales representatives that specialize in that market. The young children's toy stores will also be sold through a network of representatives with the exception of a few stores where Steve Kellar, a company cofounder, has close relationships.

Chapter 16

Company Operations and Management

O PERATIONS INCLUDES EVERYTHING YOU DO TO BUY, BUILD, PROVIDE, or procure items or services in order to offer your product or service; it also includes administration functions you require to run your company. Operations sections of business plans are dramatically different from plan to plan today, because businesses operate in so many different ways. Production is often outsourced to other companies and, in some cases, so are sales, marketing, administration, and human resource functions. For the most part, readers don't need all the information about how your operation works, but only information about the one, two, or three parts that will have a significant effect on your business. Typically, two pages on operations is a long section.

The one part of business plans that hasn't changed for years is the Management section. Good management will succeed in most businesses and bad management can turn even the best business concepts into business failures. Of course, management has to start somewhere and there have been many successful businesses started by young or inexperienced entrepreneurs. If at all possible, you want to be able to show your management has a successful background. If you don't have that experience, you need to show that management has dedication and enthusiasm and that you have found mentors who will help you.

Pitfall to Avoid

Don't assume that readers (especially investors and bankers) will believe that your success in one business is a predictor of success in another business. Each market has unique challenges and people are most interested in seeing that you have experience in the market of your current business. If you don't have that experience, do everything you can to get an employee or mentor with the proper experience. In many cases, entrepreneurs with limited experience will either have an advisory board or a board of directors of people experienced in their industry to help them.

This section shows you have thought through the different aspects of your business and that your management team is strong. As a rule, your Operations section gets a rather cursory read, but your Management section gets close scrutiny. There are two times when Operations becomes a key issue: first, when people may worry that you cannot get the key employees you need for manufacturing or technology positions, and second, when your overhead expense is so high that it threatens the survival of the company.

What to Communicate

1. **That you have minimized the company's risks.** You do this by outsourcing or having low upfront costs for production and administrative functions. You want the money going into your company to be used as much as possible for marketing, sales, and management.
2. **That your managers have experience or access to the management advisors they need to keep the company running smoothly.**
3. **That you have an effective personnel compensation plan to keep top employees and management.** This is especially true if you are recruiting employees who are difficult to find.
4. **That you have thought through the key operations issues that will affect your business.** If possible, you want to show a relationship between the resources you devote to operations and the potential sales you will have. For a new company, try to keep both management costs and overhead expenses to about 25 percent of your total expenses.
5. **That you have made a strong effort to keep your fixed costs as low as possible.** New companies especially should show they are subletting office space from an existing company or have taken other steps to keep overhead costs down. It's a red flag to investors when you want to lease

> ## Success Tip
>
> The greatest skill managers have is their ability to respond to problems. If you are short of experience, show that your management team has adjusted to problems in the past. One of the problems with the emphasis on management experience is that it implies that managers can know everything. That's not true. What they do know is how to recognize a problem and how to create a response to that problem.

expensive office or manufacturing space when you don't have enough revenue.

Format

Operations sections don't have a standard format and can discuss any relevant part of the company's operations. For your Operations section, choose the points listed here as appropriate for your business. The last three points—10, 11, and 12—refer to management. These can be broken out into a separate section, as in the Sample Section in PlayBoxes Etc., or they can be included in the Operations section.

1. **Identify the company's place of business.** Give the address and a brief description of the business.
2. **Give a short description of how goods or services are produced or procured.** Explain any outsourced operations. If goods are made by you, indicate whether your services are provided by employees or independent contractors. Give any other information that is unusual about how you produce your goods or services.
3. **If materials or services are purchased, explain the source of supply and any favorable pricing terms that you've negotiated.** This is particularly important for retail stores, for which the plan needs to detail pricing from vendors and how it compares with pricing for other area retailers. Restaurants also offer more details on procuring specialty food if that's an important part of their business.
4. **Offer a short description of any outsourced arrangements you have.** This should explain any contracts or agreements you have, pricing arrangements, and payment terms. Be sure to list clearly any favorable arrangements you have from vendors, including extended credit, a large line of credit, or amortized tooling or other cost-sharing arrangements.
5. **Explain how you've aligned your operations to keep overhead low.** This

is especially important if you have a high overhead business, like a manufacturing operation or a retail store.

6. **If you need to purchase capital equipment or you expect major computer expenses,** you should detail what those expenses are, why they are needed, and how they will help increase your bottom line.

7. **For retail stores, talk about their location—why it's advantageous, what it costs, and how it supports the company's marketing campaign.**

8. **Explain your personnel hiring and training policies.** A company's success depends greatly on the quality of the people it hires. You should explain not only how you will get the best employees, but how you will retain, train, and motivate them. This section should also include information about any stock incentives or bonus programs.

9. **Give a brief description of administrative functions, with costs.** An existing company should show administrative functions of 10 percent or less of sales revenue.

10. **List key members of your management team and provide a paragraph of information about each.** You can choose to list in the appendix complete résumés of your managers, though it is not necessary.

11. **List members of your board of directors, with a brief biography about each one's experience.**

12. **List the members of your board of advisors, if you have one.**

Section Sample—PlayBoxes Etc., Inc.

Operations

Philosophy

PlayBoxes Etc.'s approach is to concentrate on working with educators and mothers to develop creative, fun toys and selling those products through trade show attendance and a strong representative network. Production, accounting, finance, and running of the web site are all outsourced, with one administrator coordinating the activities to ensure enough product is available to fill orders.

Production

PlayBoxes Etc.'s product line is assembled and sewn by a Hmong America Opportunity Workshop in St. Paul, Minnesota. Plastic parts are currently produced in Taiwan with temporary tooling through a sourcing contact of Heather Navarro. Part of the $240,000 funds raised by the venture are to finance $20,000 in tooling costs to lower the costs of plastic injection molded parts produced in Taiwan.

Accounting and Personnel

All these will be outsourced to local providers as only 2 to 6 hours per month should be needed for these tasks.

Physical Location

PlayBoxes Etc. is subletting on a quarterly basis 200 square feet of office/warehouse space in White Bear Lake, Minnesota.

Success Tip

I recommend that every company looking for money have a board of directors, or at least a board of advisors, even if, as in the case of PlayBoxes Etc., the people have some industry experience. The board offers insight and alternative views for major decisions and forces the owner to defend his or her decisions. This added input helps protect the owner(s) from making mistakes.

Management

Management Team

Steve Kellar, company cofounder and president. Relevant experience and achievements include:

- ▶ Five years as a partner in the educational toy sales agency Kellar and Paulsen.

- ▶ Sold out partner interest to help found PlayBoxes Etc. Agency increased sales over 20 percent per year in the last three years.

- ▶ Four years as manager of the Zany Brainy store in Roseville, Minnesota. Left when the chain was purchased by F.A.O. Schwartz and ran into financial problems. Prior to Zany Brainy, worked as an administrative manager for three years at an HEP Manufacutring.

- ▶ Three years as a second-grade teacher in the Roseville, Minnesota school system.

Heather Navarro, company cofounder, product creator, and director of product development. Relevant experience includes:

- ▶ Heather has been producing play kits for four years, the first two years primarily for family and friends and the last two years at children's expos, state and county fairs, and community events. She has sold $25,000 in kits.

- ▶ Heather is a mother of three small children who play at least 10 hours per week with her playbox creations.

- ▶ Heather was a theater major at the University of Minnesota and had roles in several Minneapolis-area productions before the birth of her first child. Her love of acting started with her playing make-believe with props from her mother when she was 3 years old. She wanted to recreate that experience with her children.

Success Tip

Sometimes company founders start companies because of their passion and desire and not because of their extensive business experience. If that's the case, don't concentrate on the founder's experience, but focus on the person's passion. This is especially true when the passionate founder has a partner with appropriate experience, as is the case in PlayBoxes Etc.

Olivia Spader, administrative officer. Relevant experience includes:

- Three years as controller and office manager of Harmony Outdoor Furniture.
- Four years as purchasing agent and accountant at Sunrise Products.
- BA in Accounting, University of Minnesota.

Outside Directors

- **Tom Alagna.** Company's CPA. 18 years of experience with small to mid-sized companies, Masters in Venture Funding from the University of St. Thomas.
- **Jeremy Stern.** Former CEO of Maverick Products, a manufacturer of 14 million housewares with sales primarily to mass merchandisers, hardware stores, and small-town general merchandise stores. Seventy percent of Maverick's sales were through manufacuters' representatives.

Advisory Board

- **Edie Tolchin.** Has operated EGT Global Trading since 1997, which links U.S. inventors with Asian manufacturers to provide a "one-stop Import service" for sourcing, quality control, manufacturing, international financing, air/ocean shipping, customs clearance arrangements, and dock-to-door delivery.
- **JoAnn Hines.** Has 20+ years experience in the packaging industry, specializing in branding consumer products. She has completed packaging designs for over 60 products that have been successfully introduced into the marketplace.
- **Linda Gustafson.** Professor of Early Childhood Education at the University of Minnesota, who speaks nationwide to early childhood family educators about the importance of dramatic play in the creative development of young children.
- **Tony Steinmetz.** President of Steinmetz Associates, PlayBoxes's largest representative group with four salespeople covering Southern California. Represents PlayBoxes Etc. to both retail stores and early childhood educational centers.

Chapter 17

Financial Section

THE FINANCIAL SECTION OF THE BUSINESS PLAN IS THE KEY AREA where people will judge just how competent you are as a business manager. The financial portion of any business plan should be well written, sufficiently documented, and concise. It should follow these rules:

▶ Financial projections must tie into and be consistent with the narrative sections of the business plan—and will in a large part depend upon the stage and goals of the company.

▶ Financial projections must tie in with historical numbers and, to the extent that they do not, discrepancies should be explained. For example, if sales have been flat during the last three years, but are projected to grow at 35 percent per annum, you must explain how and why.

▶ Financials should be prepared with a specific reader or audience in mind. For example, lenders are interested in cash flow and sources of repayment, investors will focus more closely on EBITDA, and strategic

Much of the information in this chapter was furnished by Jim Lewin, BizPlanIt, 7702 E Doubletree Ranch Road, Suite 300, Scottsdale, AZ 85258, 480-970-6161, www.bizplanit.com.

partners may look at the balance sheet. (Note: this chapter assumes that the reader of the business plan is an investor or a lender.)

Buzzword

EBITDA stands for "earnings before interest, taxes, depreciation, and amortization." *Depreciation* is the amount by which you discount equipment every year it is used. *Amortization* is similar to depreciation in that you write off a major expense based on use. For example, you might amortize tooling based on production if the tool will produce only 150,000 units. A high EBITDA occurs when you have high margins and low expenses.

▶ Use charts and graphs to summarize key financial information, highlight important figures, and keep the reader interested.

▶ All financial statements should be prepared on an *accrual* basis, rather than on a *cash* basis—it shows how businesses are managed and provides the best picture for sophisticated readers. With an accrual basis, you report sales when the sale is made or an item is purchased, and not when you actually receive or pay the money. With a cash basis, businesses simply report when cash actually comes in or goes out.

What to Communicate

1. That you understand financials and the financial process. This understanding is essential if you're trying to raise money.
2. That your business will produce significant profits and that your margins are high.
3. That your business shows steady profit growth as sales increase.
4. That you will manage your finances wisely, using both your current resources and any future investments or loans.

Pitfalls to Avoid

Many entrepreneurs will have their financials prepared by a consultant or an accountant. Often the result is that they don't understand the assumptions behind the financials. It's crucial for owners to understand the assumptions, projections, and ramifications of those numbers when preparing the plan. Employing a consultant to prepare a business plan and financial projections is often helpful, but owners still need to understand their numbers.

Format

The financial portion of a business plan can often be organized into four parts:

▸ a financial review of the current/historical status of the company

▸ financial assumptions that form the basis for the projected numbers

▸ three to five years of projected financial statements

▸ an optional Financial Summary section

Financial Review

Begin with a description of the company's current financial status in which you explain the current and historical condition of the business. It is important to focus on strengths and weaknesses inherent in the numbers—particularly for areas where performance is significantly better or worse than might be expected. Explain, for instance, that a change in pricing strategy proved to be an error that resulted in a loss for the quarter, but after realizing the mistake, management reverted to its prior pricing formula. After highlighting those points that warrant discussion, provide a table to summarize key balance sheet and income statement accounts for the past three years (Figure 17-1).

	1998	1999	2000
Total Assets	$4.390	$4,788	$5,562
Stockholders' Equity	$1,998	$2,567	$3,445
Revenues	$18,920	$20,244	$22,066
Gross Profit	$9,007	$10,875	$11,342
EBITDA	$2,270	$2,456	$2,648

Figure 17-1. XYZ Company: Financial Summary

Success Tip

Boxes, graphs, or simple charts are by far the most convincing display of financial information. It is also how most other plans display financial information. Try to incorporate at least three to four boxes into your Financial section. Be sure your ratios, especially gross profits and EBITDA, are in line with the ratios of other companies in the industry. Large libraries will have reference books on standard industry ratios; the best ones are from Prentice Hall.

Financial Assumptions

Begin this section by carefully reviewing all of the underlying assumptions that form the basis of the financial projections. Like the projections, financial assumptions must be reasonable, thoughtful, and defendable. Assumptions are the numbers you use for calculating your financial statements. For example, you might assume sales will grow 10 percent per year, the cost of goods will stay at 44 percent, and sales, marketing, and administrative expenses are 22 percent of sales. State and then defend your assumptions in each section.

▶ **Sales.** Sales assumptions determine the overall level of growth for the business. Many other important assumptions will be tied into sales assumptions, such as balance sheet and cash flow assumptions. When developing sales projections for more than one product or product group, it's often useful to organize those products or groups into separate categories or line items. Similarly, if the company sells one product but in distinctly different markets, the sales should be categorized by market. This is particularly important information for a reader of your plan. Figure 17-2 shows two examples.

Revenues			Revenues	
Systems	$20,500		United States	$12,500
Software	$3,000		International	$3,000
Total Revenues	$23,500		Total Revenues	$23,500

Figure 17-2. Sales

▶ **Cost of sales.** Readers want to compare your production costs, which would be inventory cost for a retailer and cost of service personnel for a service company, to another similar company to determine if your business has efficient manufacturing or production costs.

Success Tip

Cost of goods sold should receive special emphasis in every plan, as it is an important financial figure. You can cut marketing, overhead, and administrative expenses, but it's hard to change how much it costs to produce or procure what you sell. Cost of goods sold also determines gross margin—the percentage of sales left after deducting cost of goods sold.

If a company has been in business for a number of years and knows its cost of sales run at 39 percent of sales, then future assumptions should reflect that ratio. If, on the other hand, the enterprise being planned is a start-up, or is moving into a new facility, the cost of sales must be carefully broken down into each of its components. For example, cost of sales categories might include material cost, direct labor, utilities, transportation, and overhead expenses of a manufacturing facility.

▶ **Research and development.** If there is an R&D element to the business, you need to discuss how much capital is allocated to it, usually expressed as a percentage of sales. R&D represents a company's investment in its future, so readers—particularly investors—may be quite interested in this figure.

▶ **Marketing expense.** In many younger companies, marketing expenses play a large role and early-stage investors will assume that a large portion of the capital being raised will go toward marketing to establish a brand or sell products. Heavier marketing costs are often expected for younger companies, so detail these expenses for each year of the planning period. If marketing costs are not a major expense item, they can be included with items in the next category, general and administrative expenses.

Pitfalls to Avoid

If you are a start-up, be careful to avoid adding fixed G&A expenses. For example, instead of hiring an accountant with a fixed salary, hire an outside accountant whose fees vary depending on the work level. Sales often take longer to develop than entrepreneurs expect and G&A expenses can cost a company all of its development money before sales develop.

▶ **General and administrative expenses (G&A).** Total G&A is an important figure because subtracting it from Gross Profit will determine the company's profitability. G&A consists of a number of accounts that are usually small in relation to the total, and often fixed. In the assumptions paragraph on G&A you should discuss any unusually large accounts, for example salaries, rent, or entertainment expenses. You also need to detail any significant G&A changes from historical financial performance.

▶ **Taxes.** If the plan is for a relatively mature company, then an independent accountant should be requested to prepare the tax assumptions, including topics such as type of corporation and method of accounting. If on the other hand, a company is new or emerging, a discussion of tax issues may not be relevant.

Balance Sheet Assumptions

Buzzwords

Income statements list sales less all expenses to determine income. Balance sheets show a company's assets and liabilities, both short term and long term, along with shareholders' equity. Cash flow statements show how much cash a company has on hand at any time. See Appendix A for an example of an income statement, a balance sheet, and a cash flow statement. These are the three key statements every business plan needs.

▶ **Inventory.** The assumption should include how many inventory turns are expected each year. Additionally, there should be a discussion about the relationship of inventory to cash and how practices like "just-in-time" will be utilized. This is applicable primarily for retail and manu-facturing firms.

▶ **Accounts receivable (A/R).** If you have commercial customers, it is like-ly there will be significant A/R. In this case, the assumption should advise if A/R is projected with a time period, which refers to the days you need to collect receivables, such as 60 days. Many companies that require 60 days or longer to collect payment borrow against their A/R to increase working capital. Explain any plans you have to do this in this section.

▶ **Investments.** If a company intends to raise a round of financing, this assumption will detail how funds will be invested until they are needed in the business.

▶ **Property and depreciation.** This assumption should discuss large assets the company has acquired, or expects to acquire during the planning period. It is helpful to describe how assets will be financed, if financing strategies are known. Also, advise the reader about how assets will be depreciated.

▶ **Debt.** If the company has credit facilities with banks, finance compa-nies, or leasing companies, it should be disclosed here. Information on terms, amortizations, maturity dates, collateral, and interest costs should be disclosed in this assumption.

Pitfalls to Avoid

Don't become confused by the word *assumptions* when talking about financials. In many cases, the assumptions are facts. That you have a bank loan and what the terms are certainly are facts. I've heard new entrepreneurs answer the question, "What financial assumptions have you made?" with "We haven't made any." Some parts of your Financial section are facts and other parts assumptions, but they're all called assumptions.

Financial Projections

Most business plan readers expect to see three to five years of financial projections. Less than three years is considered too short a planning period to understand a company's goals and longer than five years is often not considered to be meaningful. Financial projections should include an income statement, a balance sheet, and a cash flow statement. It's typically best to present financial projections on an annual basis, along with the prior two or three years if available, to allow readers to easily compare projections with historical performance. Many readers, particularly lenders, will also be interested in reviewing the first year or two on a monthly basis, included on separate sheets.

Many investors and banks believe that EBITDA is the best way to compare one company with another—even companies in different industries. EBITDA tells a reader how much money a company makes or loses from its operations. Therefore, it's the fairest way to evaluate a company's prospects, and I recommend that you present an EBITDA summary in a graph format in your plan (Figure 17-3).

Financial Summary

This section summarizes the overall financial results of the plan and is often included instead or also in the Executive Summary. This section may also be used to introduce other financial information that may be useful, including the following:

Financial ratios. A business plan, especially for an established company, might provide certain financial ratios for the most current year-end statements, or perhaps for all of the years during the planning period. Depending upon the type of business, certain ratios are more important than others. Some of the more widely used ratios include:

▶ **Quick ratio:** By dividing the sum of cash and accounts receivable by current liabilities, a reader can ascertain the company's liquidity. The larger the ratio, the more liquid the company is considered to be.

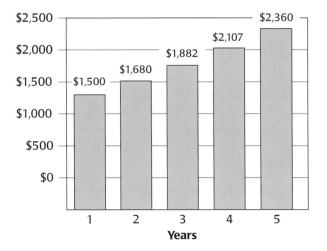

Figure 17-3. Projected EBITDA (figures in thousands)

▶ **Current ratio:** This ratio enables the reader to understand a company's ability to pay its bills. Divide current assets by current liabilities to calculate.

▶ **Total assets to net worth:** This leverage ratio varies greatly from industry to industry. However, when dividing total assets by net worth, a smaller number is always preferred—indicating the company is not too highly leveraged. The best way to judge this ratio is in comparison to other companies within a similar industry.

▶ **Collection period:** A/R divided by sales and then multiplied by 365. If the result is higher than the selling terms (say 30 days), then the company may not be effectively collecting receivables.

▶ **Net sales to inventory:** By dividing sales by inventory, the reader can analyze how efficiently a company is using its assets. Generally, the higher the number, the better.

Success Tip

An established, ongoing business will typically include these ratios because they know them from experience. For a new business these ratios are all speculation. Don't show these ratios if you can't be sure what they will be. Instead concentrate on your EBITDA and your expected sales growth. The story you want to tell is that you have a huge marketing opportunity and your gross margins will be high.

- **Assets to sales:** This ratio tells the reader if a company is gaining the most benefit from the capital that management is investing in the business.

- **Accounts payable to sales:** By dividing A/P by annual sales, a lender or supplier can determine if a company is using its suppliers to help finance operations. The lower the number, the better.

- **Return on sales:** Also known as profit margin. By dividing net profit by annual sales, the reader learns the amount of profit generated from each dollar of sales.

- **Return on assets:** Like most ratios, this one varies by industry. However, this ratio can tell the reader how efficiently a company is using assets and if it deserves additional capital to expand further.

- **Return on equity:** If the reader divides net profit by net worth, he or she can conclude if additional capital will receive an acceptable return.

Funding Request

This is a statement of the amount of money being raised and the terms of the offer; for example, a convertible note, a loan, or sale of stock.

Use of Proceeds

This section provides an opportunity to give readers further detail related to the amount and uses of capital that is either being borrowed or raised.

Exit Strategy

Investors want to know how they can get money out of an investment. Typical scenarios are an initial public offering, a merger with a larger company, or, in the case of a convertible bond or loan, terms for when the bond or loan will be repaid.

Funding Request, Use of Proceeds, and Exit Strategy are typically included in plans only when entrepreneurs are seeking money from investors.

Success Tip

Every business plan should be written with a specific audience in mind. While plans are often written to raise money, other appropriate audiences could include a company's senior management team, company employees, suppliers, strategic partners, or key customers. The Overview section of a business plan must be tailored to answer the specific questions and needs of your audience. It should be especially thorough if you are looking to borrow money from a bank.

Sample Financial Statements*

	Year 1	Year 2	Year 3	Year 4	Year 5
Revenue					
Product #1 Revenue	168,750	1,837,500	6,670,000	16,447,500	33,525,000
Product #2 Revenue	16,875	498,750	2,355,000	7,925,000	20,887,500
Service Revenue	3,000,000	6,240,000	12,480,000	24,300,000	44,400,000
Total Revenues	3,185,625	8,576,250	21,505,000	48,672,500	98,812,500
Total Cost of Sales	46,606	584,063	2,256,250	6,093,125	13,603,125
Gross Profit	3,139,219	7,992,187	19,248,750	42,579,375	85,209,375
Operating Expenses					
Employee Expenses					
Operational Payroll	2,731,511	5,089,437	7,836,488	13,709,345	19,142,322
Payroll Taxes and Benefits	819,453	1,526,831	2,350,946	4,112,804	5,742,697
Recruiting Expenses	10,000	20,000	20,000	30,000	30,000
Total Employee Expenses	3,560,964	6,636,268	10,207,434	17,852,149	24,915,019
Marketing/Sales Expenses					
Marketing Expenses	380,414	1,090,688	2,309,156	3,838,875	5,961,094
Channel Partner Fees	67,500	735,000	2,668,000	6,579,000	13,410,000
Travel/Entertainment	120,000	240,000	240,000	360,000	360,000
Total Marketing Expenses	567,914	2,065,688	5,217,156	10,777,875	19,731,094
Total Web Site and Technology	321,750	324,800	418,050	555,300	756,300
Total General and Administrative	409,740	963,156	1,926,025	3,783,724	6,935,062
Total Operating Expenses	4,860,368	9,989,912	17,768,665	32,969,048	52,337,475
Net Operating Income (EBITDA)	(1,721,149)	(1,997,725)	1,480,085	9,610,327	32,871,900

Figure 17-4. Income Statement (continued on next page)

*Prepared by BizPlanIt, *www.bizplanit.com*

	Year 1	Year 2	Year 3	Year 4	Year 5
Financial Expenses					
Depreciation	46,333	117,500	213,000	393,667	599,000
Pre-Tax Net Profit (Loss)	(1,767,483)	(2,115,225)	1,267,085	9,216,660	32,272,900
Income Taxes	0	0	0	2,508,394	12,263,702
Net Income (Loss)	(1,767,483)	(2,115,225)	1,267,085	6,708,266	20,009,198
Cumulative Net Profit (Loss)	(1,767,483)	(3,882,708)	(2,615,623)	4,092,643)	24,101,841

Figure 17-4. Income Statement (continued)

	Year 1	Year 2	Year 3	Year 4	Year 5
Assets					
Current Assets					
Cash	2,757,104	(66,834)	1,904,473	6,018,164	21,295,997
Accounts Receivable	381,747	847,959	1,866,738	4,054,979	8,215,344
Total Current Assets	3,138,851	781,126	3,771,211	10,073,143	29,511,341
Property/Equipment	193,667	436,167	713,167	1,119,500	1,690,500
Total Assets	3,332,517	1,217,292	4,484,377	11,192,643	31,201,841

Liabilities and Stockholders' Equity					
Liabilities					
Current Liabilities					
Accounts Payable	0	0	0	0	0
Total Current Liabilities	0	0	0	0	0
Total Liabilities	0	0	0	0	0
Stockholders' Equity					
Paid-in Capital	5,100,000	5,100,000	7,100,000	7,100,00	7,100,000
Retained Earnings	(1,767,483)	(3,882,708)	2,615,623)	4,092,643	24,101,841
Total Stockholders' Equity	3,332,517	1,217,292	4,484,377	11,192,643	31,201,841
Total Liabilities and Stockholders' Equity	3,332,517	1,217,292	4,484,377	11,192,643	31,201,841

Note: This model assumes that all accounts payable are paid in the month in which the expense is incurred.

Figure 17-5. Balance Sheet

	Year 1	Year 2	Year 3	Year 4	Year 5
Revenues	3,185,625	8,576,250	21,505,000	48,672,500	98,812,500
Cash Inflows					
Collection of A/R	2,803,878	8,110,038	20,486,222	46,484,258	94,652,135
Proceeds from Sale of Stock	5,100,000	0	2,000,000	0	0
Total Cash Inflows	7,903,878	8,110,038	22,486,222	46,484,258	94,652,135
Cash Outflows					
Payments on A/P	4,906,774	10,573,975	20,024,915	39,062,174	65,940,600
Payments for deposits	0	0	0	0	0
Payments to Purchase Equipment	240,000	360,000	490,000	800,000	1,170,000
Income Tax Payments	0	0	0	2,508,394	12,263,702
Total Cash Outflows	5,146,774	10,933,975	20,514,915	42,370,568	79,374,302
Net Cash Flows	2,757,104	(2,823,938)	1,971,307	4,113,691	15,277,833
Cash, Beginning of Period	0	2,757,104	(66,834)	1,904,473	6,018,164
Cash, End of Period	2,757,104	(66,834)	1,904,473	6,018,164	21,295,997

Figure 17-6. Cash Flow Statement

Financial Section Sample—PlayBoxes Etc.

Financial

Financial Review

The company has sold products at children-oriented events, fairs, and young child and young children educator events. The product has substantial testing and the five representatives who have signed on board all have seen and test-marketed the product, so the initial year's $400,000 in sales are based on substantial market research. The product has a proven 55 percent margin based on established sales and production history. The slight decrease in profitability in Year 2 is due to the hiring of a sales and marketing manager to handle sales reps and major merchants and an administrative manager. Those hiring decisions will lead to the sales increases in 2008 through 2010.

Financial Assumptions

- ▶ **Sales.**

2007	$400,000
2008	$920,000
2009	$1,530,000
2010	$2,240,000

Pitfalls to Avoid

Balance sheet assumptions are often omitted from a plan. That's a mistake, because they are an ideal summary tool for highlighting the strong points of a business concept. The PlayBoxes Etc. example quickly highlights its high margins and low marketing costs in its assumptions. I personally like to read balance sheet assumptions first, because they give the gist of whether or not a company will be profitable.

- ▶ **Cost of goods sold.** PlayBoxes Etc. gross margin is 55 percent margin.
- ▶ **Commision.** Five percent commissions paid to reps are included in marketing expenses.
- ▶ **Marketing.** Marketing and sales expenses are expected to be approximately 10 percent of sales, even with rep commissions. This is lower than the more typical 20 percent because of the use of representatives with extensive market contacts and reliance on low-cost trade show attendance.
- ▶ **General and administrative.** Rise significantly in 2008 with the addition of a Sales and Marketing Manager and an Administrative Manager.
- ▶ **Accounts receivable.** PlayBoxes Etc.'s terms are payable in 30 days, but financial forecasts use a more realistic 60-day payment cycle.
- ▶ **Accounts payable.** Sixty days after the receipt of invoice.
- ▶ **Funding request.** PlayBoxes Etc., Inc. is looking to raise $240,000 for January 2007. This would be raised by selling 240,000 shares of stock at $1 per share.

▶ **Use of proceeds.**

Permanent tooling	25,000
Setup costs for web site	20,000
Beginning kit inventory	60,000
Attendance at major trade shows	25,000
Marketing materials	15,000
Packaging design	15,000
Operating capital	80,000
Total	**240,000**

▶ **Exit Strategy.** The investors' most likely short term exit strategy is a stock or total purchase of PlayBoxes Etc. by a larger toy company, or a company stock buyback from proceeds of an SBA or traditional bank loan. Longer term, provided sales grow sufficiently, the exit strategy would be an IPO (Initial Public Offering of stock to the public.)

Exit Strategy

The company is planning either an IPO or a merger with or sale to a larger Internet consulting firm in three to four years.

	2007	2008	2009	2010
Total Revenue	$400,000	$920,000	$1,530,000	$2,240,000
Total Cost of Sales	180,000	405,000	675,000	990,000
Gross Profit	220,000	515,000	855,000	1,250,000
Total Marketing Expenses	64,000	121,667	183,333	247,333
Total Web Site and Tech Expenses	10,000	10,000	12,000	13,000
Total G&A Expenses	154,000	302,000	377,000	415,000
Total Operating Expenses	228,000	433,667	572,333	675,333
Net Operating Income (EBITDA)	−8,000	81,333	282,667	574,667
Financial Expenses	0	0	0	0
Pre-Tax Net Profit	−8,000	81,333	282,667	574,667
Income Taxes	0	20,333	70,667	143,667
Net Income	−8,000	61,000	212,000	431,000
Cumulative Net Profit	−8,000	53,000	265,000	696,000

Figure 17-1. PlayBoxes Etc. Income Statement Summary

	2007	2008	2009	2010
Assets				
Current Assets				
Cash	76,000	57,000	116,000	441,087
Accounts Receivable	66,000	155,000	255,000	375,000
Inventory				
Total Current Assets	142,000	212,000	371,000	816,087
Property/Equipment	40,000	36,000	32,000	28,000
Total Assets	182,000	248,000	403,000	844,087
Liabilities and Stockholders' Equity				
Liabilities				
Current Liabilities				
Accounts Payable	30,000	67,000	112,000	165,000
Short-Term Loans				
Total Current Liabilities	30,000	67,000	112,000	165,000
Other Liabilities				
Long-Term Loans				
Other Liabilities				
Total Other Liabilities	0	0	0	0
Total Liabilities	30,000	67,000	112,000	165,000
Stockholders' Equity				
Paid-in Capital	300,000	300,000	300,000	300,000
Retained Earnings	−148,000	−119,000	−9,000	379,087
Total Stockholders' Equity	152,000	181,000	291,000	679,087
Total Liabilities and **Stockholders' Equity**	182,000	248,000	403,000	844,087

Note: Receivables and payables paid in 60 days.
Paid-in capital includes $60,000 investment from founders that was spent by 2007.

Figure 17-8. PlayBoxes Etc. Balance Sheet Summary

	2007	2008	2009	2010
Revenues	$400,000	$920,000	$1,530,000	$2,240,000
Cash Inflow				
Receivables Paid	334,000	833,000	1,377,000	2,121,667
Investments	240,000			
Total Cash Inflows	574,000	833,000	1,377,000	2,121,667
Cash Outflow				
Cost of Goods	150,000	368,000	630,000	937,500
Mktg and Admin	228,000	433,667	572,333	675,333
Start-up Expenses	60,000			
Inventory Expense	60,000	30,000	40,000	40,000
Income Tax		20,333	70,667	143,667
Total Cash Outflows	498,000	852,000	1,318,000	1,796,500
Net Cash Flows	76,000	−19,000	59,000	325,087
Cash: Beginning of Period	0	76,000	57,000	116,000
Cash: End of Period	76,000	57,000	116,000	441,087

Figure 17-9. PlayBoxes Etc. Cash Flow Summary

Section 2
Part Two

The Business Plan:
Sample Plan

Chapter 18

Retail Store Business Plan–HydroHut

THE FINAL CHAPTER IN THIS BOOK GIVES YOU A SAMPLE BUSINESS plan—for HydroHut—that incorporporates the ideas you have read about throughout this book. It's designed to provide you with the format, language, and emphasis that will gain investors' interest from the get-go. You can use this sample plan as a model for developing your business plan. As a consultant and author, I have reviewed hundreds of plans and this one incorporates what I know will work in today's investment marketplace.

Hydro Hut

Contact Information:
HydroHut, Inc.
12709 Enfield Terrace
Austin, TX 78704
(512) 555-1212
hydrohut@internet.com
Allis Walter, President
Matthew Strang, CEO

Table of Contents

7. Management, Organization, and Ownership
Management/Principals
Organizational Structure
Professional Consultants

8. Goals and Strategies
Business Goals
Keys to Success
Future Plans

9. Financial Assumptions
Beginning Balance Sheet
Profit and Loss
Balance Sheet
Cash Plan

10. Appendix
Income Projection
Expense Projection
Profit & Loss
Balance Sheet
Cash Plan
Ratio Analysis
Personal Financial Statement
Equipment List

Note: in your plan, page numbers would be included for each section.

1. Executive Summary

HydroHut is a unique concept ready to enter the Austin, Texas retail restaurant and bar market. Its products will consist of still water drinks and baked goods for health-conscious consumers. The partners, who bring more than 12 years of retail restaurant and bar operations experience to the venture, are seeking a line of credit of $15,000 to facilitate the opening and operation of HydroHut.

Income Projections			
For years ending December 2006, 2007, and 2008			
Income Category	**Year 1**	**Year 2**	**Year 3**
Retail Walk-in	100,100	107,000	189,100
Corporate	0	8,000	13,000
Special Events	9,500	17,000	20,300
Total Income	109,600	132,000	222,400

1.1 Business Opportunity

Still (non-carbonated) water beverages are the trendiest new drinks since gourmet coffee. The market for still water drinks has been building strongly for three years and now appears ready to enter a new, accelerated period of growth.

1.2 Product/Service Description

Still water drinks are much different from the mass-produced carbonated beverages sold by the soft drink giants. They are usually produced in small quantities by entrepreneurial organizations and product quality is extremely high. Still water drinks include functional additives, including nutriceuticals, which further differentiate them from mass-market soft drinks and appeal to health-conscious consumers.

The product line, all purchased from outside vendors, will consist of approximately 20 different still water beverages and functional beverages, in addition to a selection of freshly baked breads, muffins, cookies, and other locally produced items.

1.3 Current Business Position

HydroHut will be owned by Allis Walter and Matthew Strang. The business will be structured as an equal partnership, with Mr. Walter bearing the title of President and Mr. Strang operating as Chief Executive Officer. Mr. Walter and Mr. Strang are experienced in retail restaurant bar operations.

1.4 Financial Position

Revenues of $109,600 are expected in HydroHut's first year of operations, with a 20 percent revenue increase in year two. Early in year three, a second location is planned, which will increase HydroHut's potential for success. Revenues are expected to increase considerably after the second location is opened, to $222,400. Bank financing is not expected to be required after HydroHut's first year of operation, based on the projected cash flows.

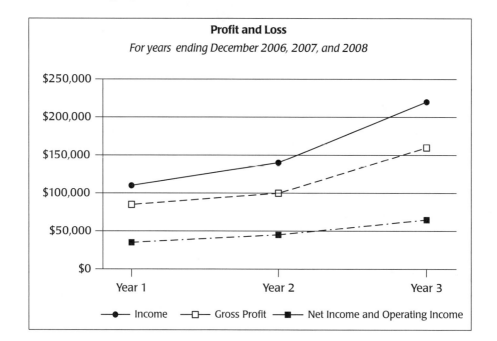

Profit and Loss
For years ending December 2006, 2007, and 2008

1.5 The Request

HydroHut is seeking to establish a $15,000 line-of-credit loan to cover start up costs, purchase needed equipment, and provide working capital until the business can support itself financially. HydroHut is requesting that this amount be formalized as a line of credit, which the company can draw from as needed.

Even though the amount requested is $15,000, HydroHut projects that it will only require funds equal to $4,250. However, such a line of credit will help HydroHut cover operating expenses should the forecast fall short. The owners are prepared to pledge personal assets in the amount of the loan to collateralize the transaction. In addition, they are willing to invest $10,000 of their own cash to help get HydroHut up and running.

2. Company Background

The two partners that will own HydroHut are Mr. Allis Walter and Mr. Matthew Strang, who together bring more than 12 years of restaurant hospitality experience to the business. The partners recognized the progressive, health-conscious lifestyles of much of Austin's population, and view the functional still water market as one with strong potential. Research of functional still water beverage locations elsewhere in the United States supported the partners' beliefs about its potential for success. There are no other such facilities in Austin at the current time.

2.1 Business Description

HydroHut will sell still water beverages through a retail outlet in Austin, Texas. The outlet will consist of a bar and seating area, as well as a service counter. It will serve beverages prepared on the premises for consumption either in the beverage bar or off-site. In addition, it will offer prepackaged products, including baked goods.

HydroHut will target its products to Austin's educated, progressive population. Austin has one of the country's highest per-capita rates of consumption of natural foods and beverages.

A retail business, including a small bar and seating area and drive-through window area, will be located in an existing facility near the intersection of Loop 1 and Enfield Road in central Austin.

2.2 Company History

Allis Walter and Matthew Strang became associated in the summer of 1996, through mutual memberships in a regional hospitality trade association. A combination of a mutual passion for health-conscious products with shared entrepreneurial attitudes eventually led them to discuss becoming business partners. After doing considerable market research in the health products industry, the partners discovered the absence of functional still water products in Austin. Further research into existing functional water facilities in the United States showed the partners the potential for success in this type of business.

2.3 Current Position and Business Objectives

HydroHut is currently in the start-up phase of its business life. The first HydroHut location will be located near Sixth Street and Lamar Boulevard, one of the city's busiest intersections and hottest retail environments. The store will be the first of its kind in Austin, a major metro area of more than 1 million people.

HydroHut's mission statement is as follows:

"HydroHut will sell still water drinks and functional beverages to health-conscious consumers in Austin, Texas. Retail customers will consist of students, faculty, and staff from the nearby University of Texas campus, the nation's largest, and residents of the well-educated, affluent surrounding neighborhoods."

Long-term goals for HydroHut include an expansion to three locations by the end of its fifth year of operations, as well as the possibility of the creation of company-owned or franchised outlets thereafter.

2.4 Ownership

HydroHut will be owned by Allis Walter and Matthew Strang. The business will be structured as an equal partnership, with Mr. Walter bearing the title of President and Mr. Strang operating as Chief Executive Officer. Mr. Walter and Mr. Strang are experienced in retail restaurant bar operations.

3. Products

Still water is the fastest growing segment of the alternative beverage industry. Sales for 1996, the most recent year available, were up 25 percent, almost double the industry average of 13 percent. Other alternative beverage segments include juices, teas, sport drinks, sparkling waters, and natural sodas.

3.1 Product Overview

The primary products to be sold through HydroHut will be functional still water drinks in three categories:

1. Nutriceuticals

Nutriceutical waters include still waters to which have been added minerals such as potassium, calcium, vitamins including A, C, and D, and other substances, such as caffeine.

2. Bacteria-Free Still Water

Bacteria-free still waters are processed using techniques that eliminate microorganisms, including associated flavors and particles, from the water.

3. Exotic Waters

Exotic waters are bottled and imported from locations such as Alaska, Canada, France, Hawaii, Sweden, and Russia.

Functional still water fountain drinks will be offered at the following prices:

Small: $1.00
Medium: $1.50
Large: $2.50

In addition, larger sizes of water will be sold for customer carryout or delivery. They will range from 1-liter bottles to 20-liter plastic jugs at prices ranging from $2.50 to $25.00.

HydroHut will sell these products, as well as prepackaged products (including baked goods), for consumption both in the beverage bar and off-site. The location will also have a drive-through window area for customer convenience.

3.2 Competitive Analysis

Currently, no other business in Austin focuses exclusively on the functional still water market. This will provide considerable flexibility in pricing and allow for the creation of a great deal of customer awareness and brand loyalty, erecting significant barriers to entry for potential competitors.

While no retail businesses devoted exclusively to functional water beverages exist in Austin, functional water beverages are sold at Whole Foods, Whole Earth Provision, Randall's Markets, and other grocery retailers.

3.3 Suppliers and Inventory

HydroHut's products will be provided by various vendors, including the following: Aqua Health, Water for Life, H2Ah!, Nutri-Water, Hydration Technologies, Guava Cool, Soft Beverages, and Millennium Moisture. These vendors supply a variety of beverages with features such as nutriceutical content, bacteria-free processing, and a number of natural, organic flavorings, including berries, fruits, and spices.

These suppliers are, for the most part, located in the continental United States. While they are not currently available for wholesale distribution in Austin, which partially explains the lack of local retail distribution, all operate existing distribution systems with representatives in other Texas cities, including Houston, San Antonio, and Dallas. No problems in obtaining adequate supplies of important products are anticipated. A projected inventory level is 30 days' worth of inventory on hand at all times.

3.4 Research and Development

HydroHut's success will come from educating customers about the appeal and benefits of functional still water beverages, and from providing a quality service and products not available in grocery stores. Price competition will be a minimal influence given current market conditions.

Expansion will begin in year three and includes the planned opening of a second location, an expansion of corporate sales, and added emphasis on special outside event promotions.

4. The Industry, Competition, and Market

HydroHut will take advantage of the rapidly growing still water beverage market niche. The market for these products has been building strongly for over three years, appealing mainly to health-conscious consumers of all age groups. While Austin, Texas contains one of the highest demographic target markets for these products, the community currently has no still water beverage retailer. The following sections discuss the opportunities for HydroHut in the Austin area.

4.1 Industry Definition

Still water is the fastest growing segment of the alternative beverage industry. Sales for 1996, the most recent year available, were up 25 percent, almost double the industry average of 13 percent. Other alternative beverage segments include juices, teas, sport drinks, sparkling waters, and natural sodas.

Still water sales totaled 731 million cases, making the category by far the dominant in alternative beverages, whose totals sales neared 1.9 billion cases. Still water's share of the alternative beverage market exceeded 39 percent, up 3.7 percent from the previous year, when 585 million cases of still waters were sold. Other strong categories included sport drinks and teas.

4.2 Primary Competitors

No other business in Austin focuses exclusively on the functional still water market. This will provide considerable flexibility in pricing and allow for the creation of a great deal of customer awareness and brand loyalty, erecting significant barriers to entry for potential competitors.

While no retail businesses devoted exclusively to functional water beverages exist in Austin, functional water beverages are sold at Whole Foods, Whole Earth Provision, Randall's Markets, and other grocery retailers.

4.3 Market Size

Austin is the capital of Texas, located near the center of the state approximately 70 miles north of San Antonio and 200 miles south of Dallas. The city has a population of roughly 500,000 and is the hub of a metropolitan area of more that 1 million people. It is home to the nation's largest university, as well as many offices related to the state government and also a booming business community, including the headquarters of Dell Computer Corp. and Whole Foods Market, the nation's largest retailer of natural foods.

4.4 Market Growth

HydroHut is an ideal business for Austin given the market including size and demographics. Based on average individual transactions of approximately $2.25, including functional still water drinks and ancillary products, the business has the potential to gross over $220,000 in sales by its third year of operation. Three additional locations are planned by the end of HydroHut's fifth year of operations.

4.5 Customer Profile

Austin has one of the highest percentages of adults possessing a college degree of any American city, and is generally regarded as the center of progressive lifestyles in the Southwest. The city has one of the nation's highest per-capita rates of consumption of natural foods and beverages. The facility will be located near desirable residential areas, the state Capitol complex, and the University of Texas main campus.

5. Marketing Plan

HydroHut's overall marketing strategy will be to educate consumers about the benefits of still water and functional water beverages, and to promote the availability through HydroHut. Customers will be reached through fliers, newspaper advertisements, publicity efforts, and special event promotions.

HydroHut will target health-conscious, progressive, and generally well-educated and affluent customers who are interested in trying new products and experiences and are dissatisfied with the limited selection and lack of personal service found in grocery store-type water retailers.

5.1 Competitive Advantage

No other business in Austin focuses exclusively on the functional still water market. This will provide considerable flexibility in pricing and allow for the creation of a great deal of customer awareness and brand loyalty, erecting significant barriers to entry for potential competitors. HydroHut will be located in a high traffic area of Austin, in the middle of its target market.

5.2 Pricing

Research in San Francisco, California, indicated that six functional still water beverage retail locations existed. The oldest has been in operation for slightly more than two years. These businesses were thriving, selling functional still water drink units at prices ranging from $1.25 for small counter-prepared beverages to be consumed on the premises, to $24.00 for larger bottles to be installed off premises in water coolers.

HydroHut's still water fountain drinks will be offered at the following prices:

Small: $1.00
Medium: $1.50
Large: $2.50

In addition, larger sizes of water will be sold for customer carryout or delivery. They will range from 1-liter bottles to 20-liter plastic jugs at prices ranging from $2.50 to $25.00.

5.3 Distribution Channels

Primary distribution of functional still water drinks will be through the retail facility, centrally located within HydroHut's target market area. Secondary distribution will consist of deliveries of bottled water beverages to restaurants, retailers, and corporate locations. The partners' previous presence in the Austin hospitality industry will contribute to HydroHut's success in the market. Additional distribution will be accomplished through temporary booths set up at athletic and cultural events, such as bicycle races and concerts.

Income by Category, Years Ending December 2006, 2007, 2008

Retail Walk-in: 85.4%

Corporate: 4.5%

Special Events: 10.1%

5.4 Promotional Plan

HydroHut will promote functional still water drinks to customers via:

Newspaper Advertisements:

Regular newspaper advertisements focusing on education and information about the benefits of functional still water beverages.

Public Relations:

A publicity campaign that will attempt to gain company owners' appearances as experts on functional still water beverages on health-related TV and radio broadcasts, and as expert sources for print publications.

Flyers:

Distributing educational and promotional fliers to residences within a one-mile radius.

Discounts:

Discounts offered to appropriate groups, such as health food cooperatives, organic gardening clubs, and cultural associations.

5.5 Feedback

When possible, HydroHut's management will conduct informal interviews with its customers. Questions regarding relative enjoyment of the products, acceptance of the product's prices, and overall satisfaction with the HydroHut experience will be asked. For corporate events, formal mail surveys will be sent to company coordinators, in order to receive feedback on how HydroHut's products were received. In addition, analysis of the effects of any marketing or promotional campaigns on immediate revenues will be performed on a case-by-case basis.

6. Operating Plan

HydroHut will be centrally located in Austin, Texas. The retail business will have a bar and seating area, as well as a drive-through window for convenience. Equipment needed will be minimal, as most of the store's products are pre-packaged. The following sections elaborate on HydroHut's operations.

6.1 Location

HydroHut will be located near the intersection of Loop 1 and Enfield Road in Austin, Texas, an attractive retail location near desirable residential areas, the state Capitol complex, and the University of Texas main campus.

In final plan picture of planned location would be here

A second location is planned to be added in the third year of operation at a suitable site to be determined.

6.2 Facility

An existing 900 square foot facility with seating and a drive-up window will be leased. Improvements will include additions to the seating area, a water bar, and landscaping.

Equipment purchased will be minimal, as the product line will be purchased from outside vendors. Baked goods will be pre-packaged and supplied from local producers.

6.3 Operating Equipment

Operating equipment needed by HydroHut primarily consists of standard restaurant fixtures. The only specialized equipment relates to the water bar, and amounts to less than $5,000 of the total capital expenditures. No future equipment is anticipated to be needed until the proposed second location is opened. HydroHut's equipment list can be found in the appendix.

6.4 Suppliers and Vendors

HydroHut's possible suppliers include Aqua Health, Water for Life, H2Ah!, Nutri-Water, Hydration Technologies, Guava Cool, Soft Beverages, and Millennium Moisture. These vendors supply a variety of beverages with features such as nutriceutical content, bacteria-free processing, and a number of natural, organic flavorings, including berries, fruits, and spices.

These suppliers are, for the most part, located in the continental United States. While they are not currently available for wholesale distribution in Austin, which partially explains the lack of local retail distribution, all operate existing distribution systems with representatives in other Texas cities, including Houston, San Antonio, and Dallas. No problems in obtaining adequate supplies of important products are anticipated.

6.5 Personnel Plan

HydroHut partners, Allis Walter and Matthew Strang, will perform the majority of the duties required to operate the initial store. One part-time employee will be hired to assist with the business.

6.6 General Operations

HydroHut will be open seven days a week, with the following hours of operation:

Monday – Friday, 10am – 10pm
Saturday, 10am – 7pm
Sunday, 12pm – 7pm

The current location is compliant with all local codes regarding accessibility for the disabled, environmental laws, and occupational safety regulations.

7. Management, Organization, and Ownership

The HydroHut partners are well experienced in the restaurant and bar hospitality industry. The partners are experienced with both customer contact tasks as well as management/operations duties. The following sections discuss the principals of HydroHut and those that they will consult with.

7.1 Management/Principals

Allis Walter has five years of experience in the retail restaurant industry. He has served as Manager of the Lava Coffee Beanery and Assistant Manager of the Travis Bagel Shop. He is a 1994 graduate of the University of Texas at Austin business school.

Matthew Strang has seven years of experience in the hospitality industry. He has served as Assistant General Manager of the Hill Country Bed & Breakfast in Fredericksburg, Texas, and Manager of Bee Cave Bar & Grill.

7.2 Organizational Structure

The business will be structured as an equal partnership, with Mr. Walter bearing the title of President and Mr. Strang operating as Chief Executive Officer. Due to the relatively small size of the initial location, the two partners will divide the day-to-day operations of the business between themselves. One part-time employee will be hired to assist operations as needed.

7.3 Professional Consultants

Due to the size of the store and the industry experience of the partners, the need to hire outside consultants should be minimal. Professional services, primarily accounting in nature, are projected to average less than $1,500 per year.

8. Goals and Strategies

HydroHut will be the first of its kind in Austin, a major metropolitan area of more than 1 million people. The store's high-quality products, marketed to Austin's health-conscious population, are expected to lead the partners to financial success.

8.1 Business Goals

HydroHut's business goals are as follows:

- ▶ To repay initial bank loans in the first year of operation.
- ▶ To open a second retail location in the third year of operation.
- ▶ To produce net income levels of over $30,000, $45,000, and $65,000 for years one, two, and three, respectively.

8.2 Keys to Success

HydroHut's success will come from educating customers about the appeal and benefits of functional still water beverages, and from providing a quality service and products not available in grocery stores. Austin has one of the highest percentages of adults possessing a college degree of any American city, and is generally regarded as the center of progressive lifestyles in the Southwest.

No other business in Austin focuses exclusively on the functional still water market. This will provide considerable flexibility in pricing and allow for the creation of a great deal of customer awareness and brand loyalty.

Customers will be reached through fliers, newspaper advertisements, publicity efforts, and special event promotions. Location will also play a crucial role in marketing and promotion. The business will be located near a high-traffic retail area in central Austin, also close to the University of Texas main campus.

8.3 Future Plans

Assuming the HydroHut concept proves successful, the owners will explore possible franchising opportunities in other cities.

HydroHut's future plans include:

- ▶ To expand to three additional retail locations by the end of year five.
- ▶ To explore additional expansion through the creation of more company-owned or, possibly, franchised outlets after year five.

9. Financial Assumptions

This section of the business plan summarizes the financial assumptions used in creating the projected financial statements (included in the Appendix).

What follows is a summary of the assumptions used to forecast the next three years of HydroHut's planned operation, including Beginning Balance Sheet, Profit & Loss, Balance Sheet, and Cash Flow data.

9.1 Beginning Balance Sheet

Beginning Balance Sheet *For year beginning January 2006*		
Assets		
Current Assets		
Cash	1,000	
Inventory	2,278	
Total Current Assets	3,278	
Fixed Assets (net)	5,000	
Other Assets (net)	8,250	
Total Assets		16,528
Liabilities		
Current Liabilities		
Accounts Payable (inventory)	2,278	
Line of Credit	4,250	
Total Current Liabilities	6,528	
Total Liabilities		6,582
Equity		
Total Equity		10,000
Total Liabilities and Equity		16,582
Debt-to-Equity Ratio		0.65

Cash. A minimum target balance of $1,000 has been set for the cash account. The partners will be infusing $10,000 into the business, and the $15,000 line of credit will be available.

Inventory. HydroHut plans on having 30 days' worth of inventory on-hand, due to the perishability of its products. Beginning inventory is calculated by looking at the total cost of sales for month 1, which is $2,278, and making sure the business has this inventory level prior to opening.

Property, Plant, and Equipment (net). This is the $5,000 of equipment HydroHut needs to buy to open its store. A detailed equipment list can be found in the appendix.

Other Assets (net). This account includes mostly intangible assets that can be amortized for accounting/tax purposes. These assets include leasehold improvements of $5,000, legal and consulting fees of $1,000, permit and licenses totaling $750, and miscellaneous start-up expenses of $1,500.

Accounts Payable. HydroHut will have Net 30 terms with its suppliers regarding inventory.

Line of Credit. Assumes a $15,000 line-of-credit loan is available, and $4,250 will be needed to fund initial start-up costs. The projected interest rate of this line of credit is 12 percent.

Contributed Cash. This is the $10,000 investment by the owners.

9.2 Profit and Loss

Profit & Loss Statement _For years ending December 2006, 2007, 2008_			
	Year 1	**Year 2**	**Year 3**
Income	109,800	132,000	222,400
Less COGS			
Material	27,305	32,590	55,007
Total COGS	27,305	32,590	55,007
Gross Profit	82,295	99,410	167,393
Operating Expenses			
Salary and Wages	7,500	8,256	25,500
Professional Services	1,500	1,100	1,300
Rent	19,596	19,596	39,204
Maintenance	900	900	1,500
Equipment Rental	1,200	1,800	2,400
Insurance	1,920	2,160	4,200
Utilities	2,160	2,160	3,900
Office Supplies	900	900	900
Postage	780	900	1,200
Marketing/Advertising	10,200	11,400	13,200
Travel	1,150	1,600	2,750
Entertainment	325	600	900
Amortization	1,650	1,650	3,025
Depreciation	1,000	1,000	1,833
Total Operating Expenses	50,781	54,022	101,812
Operating Income	31,514	45,388	65,581
Interest Expense	180	0	0
Net Income	31,334	45,388	65,581

Sales. Assumptions are based on anticipated sales for one HydroHut location, until March of the third year, when a second location is scheduled to open. Below is a breakdown summary of forecasted sales:

Income Projections For years ending December 2006, 2007, and 2008			
Income Category	**Year 1**	**Year 2**	**Year 3**
Retail Walk-in	100,100	107,000	189,100
Corporate	0	8,000	13,000
Special Events	9,500	17,000	20,300
Total Income	109,600	132,000	222,400

Cost of Sales. Calculated based on industry average information. Specifically, retail walk-in sales have a 25% cost of sales, corporate sales have a 22% cost of sales, and special event sales have a 24% cost of sales.

Salaries & Wages. Based on one planned part-time employee in years 1 & 2, with two additional part-time employees in year 3.

Marketing/Advertising. HydroHut will promote functional still water drinks to customers via newspaper advertisements, public relations activities, flyers, and group discounts.

Rent, Maintenance, Insurance, Utilities, and Travel. Reflects the higher expenses that will result from the second location opening in March of year 3.

9.3 Balance Sheet

Balance Sheet For years ending December 2006, 2007, 2008	Year 1	Year 2	Year 3
Assets			
Current Assets			
Cash	6,734	30,772	63,961
Inventory	2,730	3,065	5,785
Total Current Assets	9,464	33,837	69,746
Fixed Assets (net)	4,000	3,000	6,167
Other Assets (net)	6,600	4,950	10,175
Total Assets	20,064	41,787	86,088
Liabilities and Equity			
Current Liabilities			
Accounts Payable	2,730	3,065	5,785
Line of Credit	0	0	0
Total Current Liabilities	2,730	3,065	5,785
Total Liabilities	2,730	3,065	5,785
Equity	17,334	38,722	80,303
Total Liabilities and Equity	20,064	41,787	86,088

Cash. A minimum target balance of $1,000 has been set for the cash account. The partners will be infusing $10,000 into the business, and the $15,000 line of credit will be available.

Inventory. HydroHut plans on having 30 days' worth of inventory on-hand, due to the perishability of its products. Beginning inventory is calculated by looking at the total cost of sales for month 1, which is $2,278, and making sure the business has this inventory level prior to opening.

Property, Plant, and Equipment (net). This is the $5,000 of equipment HydroHut needs to buy to open its store. A detailed equipment list can be found in the appendix.

Other Assets (net). This account includes mostly intangible assets that can be amortized for accounting/tax purposes. These assets include leasehold improvements of $5,000, legal and consulting fees of $1,000, permit and licenses totaling $750, and miscellaneous start-up expenses of $1,500.

Accounts Payable. HydroHut will have Net 30 terms with its suppliers regarding inventory.

Line of Credit. Assumes a $15,000 line-of-credit loan is available, and $4,250 will be needed to fund initial start-up costs. The projected interest rate of this line of credit is 12 percent.

Contributed Cash. This is the $10,000 investment by the owners.

9.4 Cash Plan

Cash Plan For years ending December 2006, 2007, 2008			
	Year 1	**Year 2**	**Year 3**
Cash Receipts	109,600	132,000	222,400
Operating Cash Expenses			
Inventory Purchases	27,305	32,590	55,007
Other Expenses	48,131	51,372	96,954
Total Operating Cash Expenses	75,438	83,962	151,961
Cash from Operations	34,164	48,038	70,439
Capital Expenditures	0	0	−13,250
Debt Activities			
Interest Payments	−180	0	0
Total Debt Activities	−180	0	0
Net Cash after Capital Expenditures and Debt	33,984	48,038	57,189
Contributions	−24,000	−24,000	−24,000
Change in Cash	9,984	24,038	33,189
Beginning Cash	1,000	6,734	30,772
Cash Before Borrowing	10,984	30,772	63,961
Line of Credit Activity	−4,250	0	0
Ending Cash	6,734	30,772	63,961

Cash Receipts. Assumes sales to all customer categories will be on a cash basis. Corporate and Special Events are assumed to be collected upon completion of respective jobs, due to the limited size of HydroHut's services; however, they are still treated as cash sales.

Inventory Purchases. HydroHut plans on buying enough inventory for 30 days' sales. Based on HydroHut research, the company assumes it will be able to secure payment terms of Net 30 with its suppliers.

Other Expenses. Below is a summary of HydroHut's other expenses:

Expense Projection			
For years ending December 2006, 2007, 2008			
Expense Category	**Year 1**	**Year 2**	**Year 3**
Salaries and Wages	7,500	8,256	25,500
Professional Services	1,500	1,100	1,300
Rent	19,596	19,596	39,204
Maintenance	900	900	1,500
Equipment Rental	1,200	1,800	2.400
Insurance	1,920	2,160	4,200
Utilities	2,160	2,160	3,900
Office Supplies	900	900	900
Postage	780	900	1,200
Marketing/Advertising	10,200	11,400	13,200
Travel	1,150	1,600	2,750
Entertainment	325	600	900
Total Expenses	48,131	51,372	96,954

Distributions. Assumes a $1,000 distribution to each partner on a monthly basis for the first 3 years. Should profitability performance meet expectations, the partners may increase their monthly distribution slightly in years 2 & 3.

10. Appendix

This section contains the following reports and supporting documentation:

- ▶ Income Projection
- ▶ Expense Projection
- ▶ Profit & Loss
- ▶ Balance Sheet
- ▶ Cash Plan
- ▶ Ratio Analysis
- ▶ Personal Financial Statement
- ▶ Equipment List

This list is included for informational purposes. In the sample, these items are not shown.

Index

About the Author

Don Debelak has since 2000 been the monthly columnist of Bright Ideas for *Entrepreneur* magazine and is the author of three of the best-known invention books of the last 15 years. Don's spent his career marketing products for new and small businesses. He has also written numerous business plans for raising money, both from investors and banks. Don has worked with all types of businesses, especially as a consultant for the University of St. Thomas Small Business Center, providing advice for everything from small one-person service businesses to high-tech ventures that are set up to raise money and launch a new product. Among other books, he is author of *Perfect Phrases for Business Plans and Business Proposals*, *Successful Business Models*, *Streetwise Marketing Plan*, and *Think Big: Nine Ways to Make Millions from Your Ideas*.

Visit his Web site at **www.dondebelak.com**.

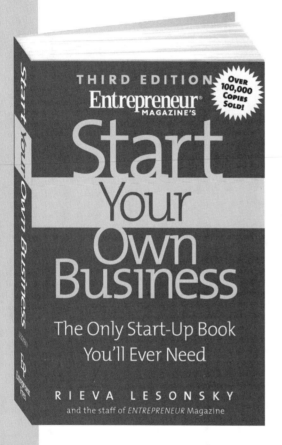